Family Circle ABZ's of Cooking

Edited by Lucy Wing with
The Family Circle Food Department

Volume 10

Introduction

A galaxy of light, crunchy, fresh salad recipes awaits you in this volume. There are salads which can be served as appetizers or first courses, main dishes or accompaniments and also fruit salads which can double as desserts.

Through the ages, fish and shellfish have provided valuable nutrients and few calories to people all over the world. Although they can be prepared by a number of different cooking methods, the secret to preparing fresh seafood is not to overcook it. The delicate flavor of most seafood goes well with herbs, sauces and other seasonings, from the simplest lemon-butter to an elegant crab-wine cream sauce. In this volume, you'll find a bounty of seafood recipes beginning with salmon, the king of fish. There are recipes using fresh, canned or smoked varieties of salmon. You will also find sardines, scallops, shrimp and sole.

A sandwich was created for the convenience of one individual. Nowadays, it's a universally popular food. You'll find classic sandwich recipes plus novel ones using croissants or pita bread. Team sandwiches with any of our soup recipes and you'll have a delicious meal!

For the time-conscious, we have included quick skillet cookery or all-in-one-pan main dishes. Add a salad and dessert and you'll have a fast dinner on the table.

Soybeans are one of the most versatile beans in the world. We Americans are just discovering their merits. Besides being made into soy sauce, soy flour or soybean oil, soybeans can be sprouted and served as a vegetable or salad, made into bean curd (tofu), or just cooked and eaten like other fresh or dried beans. Discover the versatility of soybeans!

Contents

Sabayon	579	Scrod ... 619
Sacher Torte	579	Seafood ... 619
Safflower	581	Sea Urchin ... 619
Saffron	581	Seltzer ... 619
Sage	581	Semolina ... 619
Sake	581	Sesame Seeds ... 619
Salad	581	Shad ... 620
Salad Dressing	594	Shallot ... 620
Salami	595	Shellfish ... 621
Sally Lunn	595	Sherbet ... 621
Salmon	595	Sherry ... 621
Salt	600	Shish Kebob ... 622
Sandwich	600	Shortbread ... 622
Sangria	604	Shortcake ... 623
Santa Claus Melon	604	Shortening ... 623
Sardine	604	Shrimp ... 623
Sauce	604	Skillet Cookery ... 627
Sauerbraten	608	Smelt ... 630
Sauerkraut	608	Smoked Meat ... 631
Sausage	610	Snow Pea ... 631
Sauterne	613	Sole ... 631
Savarin	613	Sorrel ... 632
Savory	613	Soufflé ... 632
Scallion	613	Soup ... 635
Scallop	613	Sour Cream ... 636
Scaloppine	617	Sourdough ... 639
Scampi	619	Soybeans ... 639
Scone	619	Soy Sauce ... 640
Scrapple	619	

Cover photo: (Clockwise from top) Provencal Tomato Dressing, page 594; Lemon French Dressing, page 594; Low-Calorie Thousand Island Dressing, page 594; Green Goddess Dressing, page 594

ISBN 0-8249-9010-2

Copyright © MCMLXXXII by The Family Circle, Inc.
All rights reserved.
Printed and bound in the United States of America.
Published by Ideals Publishing Corporation
11315 Watertown Plank Road
Milwaukee, WI 53226

Family Circle Staff

Project Editor	Lucy Wing
Food Editor	Jean Hewitt
Senior Associate Food Editor	Jane O'Keefe
Art Director	Joseph Taveroni
Copy Editor	Susan Tierney
Project Management	Annabelle Arenz
	John Jaxheimer

Ideals Publishing Staff

Project Editor	Julie Hogan
Food Stylist	Susan Noland
Photographer	Gerald Koser
Project Management	James Kuse
	Marybeth Owens

Photographs by: Avedis, Paul Christensen, Richard Jeffery, Allen Lieberman, Bill McGinn, Rudy Muller, George Nordhausen, Gordon E. Smith, Bob Stoller, Rene Velez

S

ABAYON A warm, frothy dessert consisting of eggs beaten with sugar and wine or liqueur. It is the consistency of a sauce and is often served as a dessert sauce with cake or fruit.

SACHER TORTE A rich chocolate cake, split and spread with apricot preserves, then sandwiched and iced with a bittersweet chocolate coating. One of Vienna's most famous desserts, sacher torte was created in 1832 by Franz Sacher, chef to Prince von Metternich.

SACHER TORTE

This classic cake from the Hotel Sacher in Vienna is shipped all over the world in little wooden boxes. Serve it with whipped cream.

Bake at 325° for 1 hour, 15 minutes. Makes one 8-inch cake.

Almond Praline
(recipe follows)
6 eggs, separated
½ cup sugar
½ cup (1 stick) butter or margarine, softened
1 package (6 ounces) semisweet chocolate pieces, melted and cooled
¾ cup *sifted* cake flour
1 teaspoon baking powder
1 jar (12 ounces) apricot preserves
Chocolate Glaze *(recipe follows)*

1. Make Almond Praline. Grease an 8 × 3-inch springform pan. Preheat oven to 325°.
2. Beat egg whites in a large bowl with electric mixer at high speed until foamy-white. Sprinkle in ⅓ cup of the sugar, 1 tablespoon at a time, beating all the time until meringue forms soft peaks.
3. With same beaters, beat butter until soft in a small bowl; add remaining sugar and egg yolks; beat until light and fluffy, about 3 minutes. Beat in chocolate and ½ cup Almond Praline at low speed; gently fold into egg whites. Sift flour and baking powder over bowl; fold in just until blended. Pour into prepared pan.
4. Bake in a preheated slow oven (325°) for 1 hour and 15 minutes or until cake tester inserted into center comes out clean. Cool 10 minutes in pan on wire rack. Loosen around edge; remove ring from pan; cool completely.
5. Even off top, then split cake horizontally into 2 layers. Spread about ½ of the preserves on bottom layer; replace top. Brush or spread remaining preserves on top and side of cake. Let stand at least 2 hours for preserves to soak in and partially dry.
6. Prepare Chocolate Glaze and pour over top of cake, letting it drip down side, smoothing with a warm spatula. Reserve about 2 tablespoons glaze to drizzle over top. Sprinkle top with reserved praline powder. Drizzle reserved glaze from a wax paper cone over praline. Serve with whipped cream.

Almond Praline: Heat ⅓ cup sugar in small skillet just until melted and starting to turn golden in color. Add ⅓ cup slivered almonds. Continue heating over medium heat until almonds start to "pop" and mixture is deep golden. Pour onto buttered cookie sheet. Cool completely. Break into smaller pieces and crush finely in blender or with rolling pin. Makes about ¾ cup.

Chocolate Glaze: Blend 2 tablespoons water, 2 tablespoons light corn syrup and 1½ cups 10X (confectioners') sugar in medium-size bowl; stir in 1½ squares unsweetened chocolate. Set bowl over hot, not boiling, water; heat, stirring often, until chocolate melts and glaze is thin enough to pour over the cake. Makes about 1 cup.

● ● ●

Salad

SAFFLOWER A thistle-like plant from which a vegetable oil and natural dye are extracted. The oil is obtained from the seeds; the dye comes from its reddish-orange flowers. For centuries the plant has been grown in India, the Middle East and Africa. It is now cultivated in the United States and southern Europe.

Safflower oil is clear and flavorless. It is available bottled and sold in supermarkets or may be blended with other vegetable oils, then bottled.

The orange dye from the flowers is used to color fabric in the Orient. The flowers themselves can be used to color foods. They are sometimes sold as saffron which is somewhat similar. Also called bastard saffron.

SAFFRON One of the world's most expensive spices, saffron is the dried stigma of a purple crocus flower. The crocus plant, which is about 6 inches high, was believed native to the Near East and transplanted to Spain where most, and the best, of the world's supply is produced.

The reddish-yellow stigmas, which grow three per flower, resemble dried threads or filaments. They are hand-harvested and it takes about 225,000 stigmas to make 1 pound, which accounts for its high price. However, only a small pinch is needed in a recipe to color or flavor the food.

Available as whole threads or ground, saffron gives cakes, breads and rice a bright yellow color. When used with other foods, it imparts a distinct flavor.

SAGE A popular herb for seasoning pork, sage can also add its aromatic flavor to poultry, eggs, soups, cheese spreads and stuffing. Sage is commercially grown in California, Oregon and Washington from plants introduced from Dalmatia, Yugoslavia. With over 400 varieties of sage available, Dalmatian sage is one of the best. The home garden variety, *Salvia officinalis,* is a shrubby perennial plant with gray-green, elongated, oval leaves. Fresh sage, sold in some markets, is usually the home garden variety. Dried sage is sold either rubbed or ground. See also **HERBS.**

SAKE A Japanese liquor made from rice which is cleansed, steamed and fermented. Sake is colorless and sweet with a bitter aftertaste. Usually served warm in porcelain cups. It is 12 to 16 percent alcohol by volume.

SALAD A salad, perhaps more than any other type of food, can be served as any course of a meal. Tart, marinated vegetables, dished up in small portions, make splendid first courses. Frilly, green, delicately dressed salads accompany meats to perfection. A salad made with meats, poultry, eggs, seafood or cheese becomes the main course. A salad laden with fruit and enriched with cream or yogurt can easily double as dessert.

The word "salad" is derived from *sal,* the Latin word for salt. Salt was used in the early days not only to flavor edible plants but to preserve plants for eating during the winter when they were not available.

How to Make a Perfect Jellied Mold

Mixing: Follow directions carefully when dissolving gelatin, as mixture should be sparkling-smooth, with no tiny granules clinging to the bowl.

Fruit-flavored gelatin will dissolve quickly in hot water. Unflavored gelatin can be dissolved either of these ways: (1) Soften in cold water, then dissolve in a hot liquid—or heat softened gelatin over hot water (as in a double boiler) until dissolved; or (2) mix dry gelatin with sugar, then add liquid; heat, following specific recipe directions.

Chilling: Place dissolved gelatin in the refrigerator to chill until syrupy-thick (consistency should be like an unbeaten egg white). Gelatin sets first at the bottom and sides of the bowl, so stir occasionally for even thickening.

In a hurry? Follow suggestions on package label or hasten setting either of these ways: (1) Pour the gelatin mixture into shallow pan and place in refrigerator. (2) Set bowl of gelatin mixture in a larger bowl of ice and water. Keep on the kitchen counter where you can watch it, as it gels fast.

Gelatin set too quickly? Place the bowl over simmering water and heat, stirring constantly, until melted. Then start chilling again, as if it were freshly mixed.

Layering: Like a fancy design on the top? Place mold in a larger pan of ice and water (the pan should be deep enough so the ice and water will come to within one inch of top of mold). Spoon about a ¼-inch-thick layer of syrupy gelatin into a mold and chill just until beginning to be sticky-firm. Arrange foods to make the design you wish on top of it; carefully spoon on another thin gelatin layer barely to cover; chill just until sticky-firm. This is important whenever you add one layer on top of another, so layers will hold together. This way a layered mold will turn out beautifully firm without one layer slipping from another.

Make any remaining layers this way: Keep rest of gelatin syrupy-thick. (On a cool day keep it at room temperature, or watch it if it is necessary to keep it refrigerated.) Fold in other recipe ingredients, then spoon mixture carefully on top of the already-set layer while it is still sticky-firm.

Setting: Place mold in a far corner of your refrigerator where it can chill without being disturbed. Most molds can be turned out at their prettiest if chilled overnight. Large ones, or those heavy with fruits or vegetables, need at least 12 hours' chilling. Usually, small molds are firm enough to turn out after 3 or 4 hours chilling.

How to Make Perfect Green Salads
● Begin with chilled, crackly-crisp greens. Use more than one variety: dark with light; mild with tangy.
● Tear, rather than cut, greens into bite-size pieces.
● Choose the salad dressing carefully. A thin French or Italian dressing goes well with plain or mixed greens, as does a simple oil and vinegar dressing.

Pictured opposite: Sacher Torte, page 579

Overleaf: (Clockwise from top) Sunset Salad, page 590; Shrimp and Cantaloupe Salad, page 586; German Potato Salad, page 591

ABZ's of Cooking 581

A GALLERY OF SALAD GREENS

From crunchy iceberg to peppery cress, here are the tossings of superb salads. For contrasts, toss two together. Better yet, three.

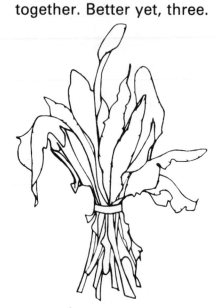

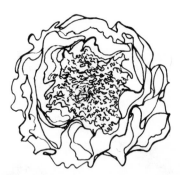

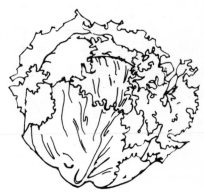

Chicory (Or **Curly Endive**) Sprawling, frilly, green head, sharp flavor, medium-crisp. Season: Year-round.

Watercress Has peppery, medium-crisp, medium-green leaves branching from slender stalks. Season: Year-round.

Boston Lettuce Also known as **Butterhead.** Soft, loose head; tender, delicate leaves ranging from yellow to green. Season: Year-round.

Sorrel Also known as **Dock.** Bright green, tongue-shaped leaves, pleasantly sour in flavor. Season: Year-round.

Romaine Also known as **Cos Lettuce.** Cylindrical, medium-green head with crisp, delicate leaves. Season: Year-round.

Field Salad Also known as **Lamb's Quarter.** Dark-green, small, spoonlike leaves with radish-sharp flavor. Season: Fall, winter.

Bibb Lettuce Also known as **Limestone Lettuce.** The tiny dark-green heads have buttery leaves. Season: Year-round.

Iceberg Lettuce Compact, crisp head with pale to medium-green leaves. Season: Year-round.

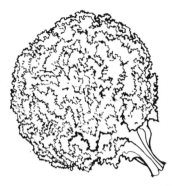

Leaf Lettuce Also known as **Garden Lettuce**. Has sprawling, ruffled leaves; pale green and delicate. Season: March-July.

Belgian Endive Small, chunky, ivory-hued heads with mellow to bitter flavor. Softly crisp, but not crunchy. Season: Fall-spring.

Chinese Cabbage Also called **Celery Cabbage**. Has tight, long, pale-green to ivory head. Delicate. Season: Year-round.

Escarole A cross between leaf lettuce and chicory. Curly green leaves, medium-crisp, mildly bitter flavor. Season: Year-round.

Fennel Also called by Italian name **Finocchio**. Bulbous, pearly-white stalk, feathery green tops, licorice flavor. Season: Fall-spring.

MAIN DISH SALADS

VEGETABLE CHEESE SALAD

Lima beans, zucchini and carrot are topped with crunchy walnuts and an herbed yogurt dressing.

Makes about 4 servings.

- ¾ **pound small, firm zucchini, trimmed**
- ¾ **pound carrots, pared (about 5 or 6 medium-size)**
- 1 **package (10 ounces) frozen baby lima beans**
- 1 **teaspoon salt**
- 2 **tablespoons lemon juice**
- ¼ **teaspoon leaf marjoram, crumbled**
- ¼ **teaspoon leaf thyme, crumbled**
- ¼ **teaspoon pepper**
- 1 **small clove garlic, minced**
- 1¼ **cups plain yogurt**
- 1 **package (6 ounces) feta or Swiss cheese, cubed**
- ¾ **cup coarsely chopped walnuts**

1. Drop zucchini and carrots into a large saucepan of boiling water. Cook 5 minutes or just until slightly softened. Remove from water; run under cold water; chill.
2. Combine the lima beans in a saucepan with ½ teaspoon of the salt and ½ cup water; cook gently, covered, until just tender; about 10 minutes. Drain, if necessary, and chill.
3. Combine lemon juice, remaining ½ teaspoon salt, marjoram, thyme, pepper and garlic. Stir into the yogurt and chill for at least 1 hour.
4. Cut the zucchini in half crosswise; cut each piece in half lengthwise. Place, flat-side down; cut each quarter into 4 lengthwise strips.
5. Cut the carrots in half crosswise; cut each piece in half lengthwise; place, flat-side down; cut lengthwise into neat strips.
6. Toss the lima beans with the cubed cheese.
7. Arrange all the vegetables on a platter; spoon the yogurt dressing over all and sprinkle with the chopped walnuts.

Salad

SHRIMP AND CANTALOUPE SALAD

Makes 4 servings.

- 1 large cantaloupe
- 1 small ripe avocado
- 3 tablespoons lemon juice
- ¾ pound raw shrimp, shelled, deveined and cooked
  - OR: ½ pound frozen shelled and deveined shrimp, cooked
- ½ cup sliced water chestnuts
- ½ cup vegetable oil
- 2 tablespoons vinegar
- 2 tablespoons chopped bottled chutney
- ¼ teaspoon salt
- ¼ teaspoon curry powder
  Pinch pepper
  Romaine leaves

1. Quarter cantaloupe; scoop out seeds. Loosen fruit from rind with a grapefruit knife; cut loosened fruit into 6 crosswise slices.
2. Halve, pit and peel avocado; cube into a medium-size bowl. Sprinkle cubes with 1 tablespoon of the lemon juice. Add shrimp and water chestnuts; toss lightly; chill.
3. Combine oil, vinegar, chutney, salt, curry powder, pepper and remaining lemon juice in a small bowl; mix well.
4. To serve: Arrange cantaloupe on romaine leaves; spoon shrimp mixture over cantaloupe; spoon dressing over salad.

THE PERFECT CHEF'S SALAD

You can vary this recipe by substituting ham or turkey for the chicken, and Swiss or Cheddar for the blue cheese.

Makes 6 servings.

- 2 whole chicken breasts
- 3 cups torn Boston lettuce
- 3 cups torn romaine leaves
- 1 cup sliced celery
- 6 bacon slices
- 1 ripe avocado
- 1 tablespoon lemon juice
- 2 tomatoes, cut into thin wedges
- 3 hard-cooked eggs, sliced
- 4 ounces blue cheese, crumbled
  Herb Vinaigrette Dressing *(recipe follows)*

1. Cook chicken by boiling in water, broiling or microwaving; cool. Skin and bone; chill; then cut into thin slices.
2. Combine lettuce, romaine and celery in a large bowl; cover; refrigerate.
3. Cook and crumble bacon.
4. Halve avocado; peel and pit. Cut into cubes; sprinkle with lemon juice.
5. Place tomatoes, avocado, chicken, bacon, eggs and cheese over greens.
6. Pour ⅓ of the Herb Vinaigrette Dressing over the salad just before serving; toss gently to coat. Pass the rest of the dressing.

HERB VINAIGRETTE DRESSING

Makes 1¼ cups.

- ¾ cup vegetable oil
- ½ cup tarragon-flavored vinegar
- ¾ teaspoon salt
- ¼ teaspoon seasoned pepper
- ¼ teaspoon leaf basil, crumbled

Place all ingredients in a jar with a tight-fitting lid. Cover. Refrigerate to mellow flavors. Shake just before pouring over salad.

CHICKEN AND CHERRY TOMATO SALAD WITH AVOCADO DRESSING

Makes 4 servings.

- 2 tablespoons lemon juice
- ½ teaspoon salt
- ½ teaspoon sugar
- 2 teaspoons leaf basil, crumbled
- 2 dashes liquid hot pepper seasoning
- 1 small very ripe avocado
- 1 green onion, minced
- ⅓ cup olive oil
- 3 to 4 cups cubed cooked chicken
- 1 head Bibb lettuce
- 1 pint cherry tomatoes, halved

1. Combine lemon juice, salt, sugar, basil and hot pepper seasoning in a cup. Peel, pit and mash the avocado with a fork in a small bowl and gradually stir in the lemon juice mixture and the onion. Slowly beat in the oil with a fork or whisk.
2. Toss the chicken with the dressing and spoon it into the center of a platter. Arrange the lettuce around the edge. Surround the chicken with tomatoes.

RIO-RANCHO SUPPER SALAD

Two varieties of canned beans plus crunchy fresh vegetables make this a hearty main dish.

Makes 6 servings.

- 1 can (16 ounces) chick-peas, drained
- 1 can (16 ounces) red kidney beans, drained
- 1 can (6 ounces) pitted ripe olives, drained
- 1 cup sliced green onions
- ½ cup chopped fresh parsley
- 1 to 2 cloves garlic, finely chopped
- ¾ cup Home-Style Tomato Dressing *(recipe follows)*
- 1 package (8 ounces) Monterey Jack or Cheddar cheese, diced (2 cups)
- 1 cucumber, pared, seeded and diced
  Chicory
- ¼ pound sliced salami or other cold cuts
- 2 ripe tomatoes, cut into wedges
  OR: 1 pint cherry tomatoes

1. Combine chick-peas, kidney beans, olives, green onions, parsley, garlic and dressing in large bowl; chill several hours.
2. Just before serving, stir in cheese and cucumber. Line salad bowl with chicory; mound bean mixture on top.
3. Fold salami slices and arrange around edge with tomatoes. Serve with crusty bread, if you wish.

HOME-STYLE TOMATO DRESSING

Makes about 3 cups.

- 1 can (8 ounces) tomato sauce
- ½ cup red wine or cider vinegar
- 1 small onion, cut up
- 2 tablespoons brown sugar
- 2 tablespoons Worcestershire sauce
- 1 teaspoon salt
- 1 teaspoon paprika
- ¼ teaspoon pepper
- 1 cup vegetable oil

1. Combine all ingredients except oil in the container of an electric blender; cover and whirl until smooth.
2. Add oil gradually; continue blending until thickened and smooth.

Pictured opposite: Chicken and Rotelle Salad, page 589

Salad

RICE, HAM AND APPLE SALAD WITH DILL MUSTARD DRESSING

Makes 4 servings.

1½ cups uncooked long-grain rice
  1 tablespoon white wine vinegar
  1 tablespoon Dijon mustard
  2 tablespoons lemon juice
  1 teaspoon salt
  ½ teaspoon pepper
  ½ cup olive oil
  1 pound cooked ham, cut ¼-inch thick
  ¼ cup thinly sliced green onions
  3 tablespoons finely snipped fresh dill
    OR: 1 tablespoon dillweed
  ⅓ cup minced fresh parsley
1½ cups diced, unpared, tart green apples (2 medium-size)
    Leaf lettuce

1. Cook the rice following label directions. Remove pan from heat; let stand while preparing the dressing.
2. Combine vinegar, mustard, lemon juice, salt, pepper and olive oil in a jar with a tight-fitting lid; cover; shake.
3. Cut ham into ¼ × 1½-inch strips. Pour dressing over ham, onions and dill in a large bowl. Toss cooked rice with a fork to separate grains; add to bowl. Add parsley and toss salad gently to coat rice. Refrigerate 2 hours until thoroughly chilled.
4. When ready to serve, add the apples; toss again. Spoon into a lettuce-lined salad bowl.

MEDITERRANEAN TUNA SALAD

Makes 6 servings.

  ¼ cup tarragon-flavored vinegar
  2 tablespoons lemon juice
  1 clove garlic, minced
  2 tablespoons chopped fresh parsley
  ½ teaspoon leaf basil, crumbled
  ½ teaspoon salt
  ⅛ teaspoon pepper
  ½ cup olive oil
1½ pounds new red potatoes
  1 cup sliced celery
  2 cans (7 ounces each) tuna, drained and broken into chunks
  1 jar (7 ounces) roasted red peppers

  2 hard-cooked eggs, cut into wedges
  1 can (2 ounces) flat anchovy fillets, drained
    Lettuce leaves

1. Combine vinegar, lemon juice, garlic, parsley, basil, salt, pepper and oil in a jar with a tight-fitting lid; cover; shake until well mixed.
2. Wash potatoes well in cold water; cook in boiling water 20 minutes or until tender. Drain; cool, then slice. (Peel potatoes before slicing, if you wish.) Place potatoes and celery in a shallow bowl; pour dressing over; toss gently to coat potatoes well. Refrigerate and allow to marinate at least 2 hours. Refrigerate tuna, peppers, eggs and anchovies separately.
3. To serve: Line a deep platter or shallow bowl with lettuce leaves. Lift potatoes from dressing and arrange on top of lettuce; reserve dressing. Top with tuna, peppers and eggs. Arrange anchovies on top; drizzle with reserved dressing.

FRANKFURTER AND 4-BEAN SALAD

Makes 12 servings.

  1 package (1 pound) frankfurters, sliced ¼ inch thick
  1 can (20 ounces) chick-peas, drained
  1 can (16 ounces) red kidney beans, drained
  1 can (16 ounces) green lima beans, drained
  1 can (16 ounces) cut green beans, drained
  1 cup chopped celery
  1 medium-size onion, chopped (½ cup)
  ⅓ cup vegetable oil
  3 tablespoons vinegar
  1 clove garlic, minced
  1 tablespoon salt
  ½ to 1 teaspoon crushed red pepper
  ¾ cup dairy sour cream
1½ tablespoons prepared mustard
    Leaf lettuce
  2 tomatoes, cut into wedges

1. Place frankfurters, chick-peas, kidney beans, lima beans, green beans,

celery and onion in a large bowl.
2. Combine oil, vinegar, garlic, salt and pepper in a 1-cup measure; stir to mix. Pour over frankfurters and beans; toss gently to coat. Cover. Chill 2 to 3 hours.
3. Just before serving, combine sour cream and mustard; fold into frankfurter-bean mixture. Line large salad bowl with lettuce; spoon salad into bowl; ring with tomato wedges.

REUBEN CHEF'S SALAD

Makes 4 servings.

  1 can (27 ounces) sauerkraut
  1 cup shredded carrots
  ½ cup chopped green pepper (½ medium)
  ½ cup chopped fresh parsley
  1 package (8 ounces) sliced corned beef
  1 package (6 ounces) sliced Swiss cheese
    Rye Croutons (recipe follows)
  ½ cup mayonnaise
  2 tablespoons chili sauce
  1 tablespoon milk
  1 green onion, chopped

1. Drain sauerkraut; rinse with cold water; drain again. Combine with carrots, green pepper and parsley in a medium-size bowl. Cover; refrigerate until well-chilled.
2. Cut corned beef and Swiss cheese into julienne strips.
3. Just before serving, place half of sauerkraut mixture in large salad bowl; top with half the Rye Croutons. Repeat layers. Arrange corned beef and Swiss cheese on top.
4. Combine mayonnaise, chili sauce, milk and green onion; pour over salad; toss to mix.
Rye Croutons: Cut 3 slices rye bread into small cubes; toss with 2 tablespoons melted butter in a shallow baking pan. Bake in a hot oven (400°) for 10 minutes, stirring once or twice.

TOMATO RING WITH EGGS AND CURRIED HERRING SALAD

Makes 12 servings.

  2 envelopes unflavored gelatin
3½ cups tomato juice
  3 tablespoons tomato paste

⅓ cup lemon juice
2 teaspoons Worcestershire sauce
¼ teaspoon salt
Lettuce
Eggs Romanoff *(recipe follows)*
Curried Herring Salad *(recipe follows)*

1. Sprinkle gelatin over 1 cup of the tomato juice in a large saucepan; let stand 5 minutes to soften. Heat, stirring often, until gelatin is dissolved; remove from heat.
2. Blend in tomato paste, lemon juice, Worcestershire sauce, salt and remaining tomato juice. Pour into a 4-cup ring mold. Chill several hours or until firm. Loosen gelatin around top of mold with tip of knife. Dip mold in and out of hot water.
3. Center over serving platter. Unmold. Garnish with lettuce and Eggs Romanoff. Spoon Curried Herring Salad into center.

EGGS ROMANOFF

Makes 12 servings.

6 hard-cooked eggs
½ cup mayonnaise
1 teaspoon Dijon mustard
Red and black lumpfish caviar

Halve eggs lengthwise. Press egg yolks through a fine sieve into a small bowl. Add mayonnaise and mustard; blend well. Stuff yolk mixture into whites. Garnish tops with red and black lumpfish caviar.

CURRIED HERRING SALAD

Makes 12 servings.

2 jars (8 ounces each) pickled herring in wine sauce, drained
¾ cup mayonnaise
½ cup dairy sour cream
1 teaspoon prepared mustard
2 teaspoons curry powder
¼ teaspoon salt
2 red apples, quartered, cored and diced (2 cups)
1 medium-size onion, diced (½ cup)

1. Dice herring pieces, reserving a few pieces for garnish.
2. Blend mayonnaise, sour cream, mustard, curry powder and salt in

large bowl. Fold in herring, apples and onion. Chill several hours.
3. To serve: Spoon salad into the center of the tomato aspic ring. Garnish with strips of reserved herring.

CHICKEN AND ROTELLE SALAD

Makes 8 servings.

1 broiler-fryer (about 3 pounds), cut up
1 package (1 pound) rotelle (spiral pasta)
1 cup olive oil
4 cups fresh parsley leaves
¼ cup pine nuts (pignolias) or walnuts
2 large cloves garlic, minced
1½ teaspoons leaf basil
1 teaspoon salt
½ cup grated Parmesan cheese
Romaine leaves
1 pint cherry tomatoes, cut into halves
¼ cup pitted ripe olives

1. Simmer chicken in water to cover in a large saucepan until tender, about 40 minutes; cool. Skin, bone and cut into strips. Cover and refrigerate.
2. Cook rotelle following label directions; drain. Rinse with cold water; drain again; turn into large salad bowl.
3. Combine olive oil, parsley, pine nuts, garlic, basil and salt in the container of an electric blender; cover and whirl until parsley is finely chopped. Pour into a small bowl; stir in cheese. Edge salad bowl with romaine leaves.
4. Toss rotelle with half the dressing; mound chicken in center of bowl; edge bowl with tomatoes and olives. Serve at room temperature with remaining dressing.

ACCOMPANIMENT SALADS

CARROT SALAD IN LEMON AND MUSTARD DRESSING

Makes 4 servings.

¼ cup lemon juice
2 teaspoons Dijon mustard
2 teaspoons sugar
½ cup minced green onions

6 tablespoons olive or vegetable oil
½ teaspoon salt
⅛ teaspoon freshly ground pepper
2 tablespoons snipped fresh dill
OR: 2 teaspoons dillweed
6 carrots, scraped and cut in julienne strips
3 cups water
Pinch salt
1 teaspoon sugar

1. Combine lemon juice, mustard, the 2 teaspoons sugar, green onions, oil, the ½ teaspoon salt, pepper and dill in a jar with a tight-fitting lid. Cover. Shake until well blended.
2. Combine carrots with water to cover in a large saucepan; add remaining salt and sugar. Bring to boiling; lower heat; cover. Simmer 5 minutes or until tender. Don't overcook. Drain, then cool under running cold water; drain again and transfer to a salad bowl.
3. Pour dressing over; toss lightly. Taste; add additional seasoning, if needed. Chill at least 2 hours, but remove from the refrigerator about 30 minutes before serving.

CAULIFLOWER SALAD

Makes 8 servings.

1 medium-size cauliflower
2 medium-size zucchini
⅔ cup bottled oil-and-vinegar dressing
Leaf lettuce
Canned pimiento

1. Separate cauliflower into flowers; wash well. Trim zucchini and cut into thin slices.
2. Cook vegetables in boiling salted water in separate saucepans for 10 minutes or just until crisp-tender. Remove vegetables with a slotted spoon to a large shallow glass dish and arrange in separate mounds. Pour bottled dressing over; cover. Chill several hours to blend flavors.
3. Line salad bowl with leaf lettuce; arrange a ring of cauliflower around edge and fill center with zucchini; garnish with pimiento cut into star shapes, if you wish.

Salad

COLESLAW WITH PINEAPPLE AND ORANGE

Makes 4 servings.

- **1 small head cabbage (1 pound)**
- **1 can (8 ounces) pineapple chunks in pineapple juice, drained and halved**
- **1 large navel orange, pared and sectioned**
- **½ cup dairy sour cream**
- **2 tablespoons lemon juice**
- **3 teaspoons drained prepared horseradish**
- **1 teaspoon sugar**
- **¾ teaspoon salt**
- **½ teaspoon dry mustard**

1. Trim cabbage of the outer leaves; quarter and core; shred. (You will need about 6 cups.) Combine cabbage with pineapple and orange sections in a large bowl.
2. Blend sour cream, lemon juice, horseradish, sugar, salt and dry mustard in a small bowl. Pour dressing over cabbage mixture and toss to coat. Cover; refrigerate several hours. Toss again before serving.

BEAN SPROUTS AND TOMATO SALAD

Makes 4 servings.

- **1 can (16 ounces) bean sprouts, rinsed and drained**
- **1 cup cherry tomatoes, cut into halves**
- **½ cup seeded and slivered cucumber**
- **½ cup chopped fresh parsley**
- **3 tablespoons olive or vegetable oil**
- **1 tablespoon red wine vinegar**
- **½ teaspoon salt**
- **⅛ teaspoon pepper**
- **¼ teaspoon leaf basil, crumbled Pinch paprika**
- **1 large clove garlic, crushed**

1. Toss bean sprouts, tomatoes, cucumber and parsley together in a bowl. Cover; refrigerate 30 minutes.
2. Measure oil, vinegar, salt, pepper, basil and paprika into a cup or bowl; add crushed garlic. Blend with a wire whisk.
3. Just before serving, pour dressing over salad; mix lightly. Spoon onto 4 chilled salad plates. Garnish with fresh parsley, if you wish.

SPINACH WATERCRESS SALAD

Makes 8 servings.

- **1 package (10 ounces) fresh spinach**
- **1 large bunch watercress**
- **1 head Bibb lettuce**
- **¼ pound mushrooms, thinly sliced**
- **6 tablespoons olive oil**
- **2 tablespoons lemon juice**
- **1 clove garlic**
- **1 egg yolk**
- **1 tablespoon dry sherry**
- **1 teaspoon Dijon mustard**
- **½ teaspoon sugar**
- **½ teaspoon salt**
- **⅛ teaspoon freshly ground pepper**

1. Remove any large stems from spinach; wash leaves; drain well, then tear into bite-size pieces. (You should have 12 cups.) Place in large salad bowl. Wash and pick over watercress; remove tough stems; tear into bite-size pieces and add to spinach in bowl. Wash and trim Bibb; drain well, then tear into pieces; add to bowl along with mushrooms.
2. Combine remaining ingredients in the container of an electric blender; cover; whirl until smooth. Just before serving, toss salad with dressing to coat evenly.

GARDEN GREENS WITH BUTTERMILK DRESSING

The piquant dressing has only 12 calories per serving.

Makes 4 servings.

- **½ cup buttermilk**
- **½ clove garlic, mashed**
- **¼ teaspoon sugar**
- **¼ teaspoon dry mustard**
- **¼ teaspoon salt**
- **⅛ teaspoon pepper**
- **1 quart salad greens (chicory, romaine, watercress and Boston lettuce)**
- **1 cucumber, pared and sliced**
- **4 radishes, sliced**
- **4 ounces Swiss cheese, cut into matchstick pieces**

1. Combine buttermilk, garlic, sugar, mustard, salt and pepper in a measuring cup. Stir to mix well.
2. Wash, dry and tear the salad greens into pieces. Place in a salad bowl with cucumber, radishes and cheese.
3. Pour dressing over; toss to coat.

BIBB LETTUCE MIMOSA

Makes 8 servings.

- **4 heads Bibb lettuce**
- **OR: 2 heads Boston lettuce**
- **2 hard-cooked eggs, finely chopped**
- **Creamy Italian Dressing (recipe follows)**

Wash lettuce; dry on paper toweling. Remove outer leaves of Bibb lettuce; line salad bowl. Cut hearts of lettuce into 4 or 6 wedges through core. Arrange spoke-fashion over bed of lettuce in bowl. Sprinkle with chopped eggs. Ladle some of dressing over salad; pass remainder at table.

CREAMY ITALIAN DRESSING

Makes about 1½ cups.

- **1 egg**
- **1 tablespoon Dijon mustard**
- **½ small onion**
- **½ teaspoon salt**
- **¼ teaspoon pepper**
- **1 clove garlic**
- **⅛ teaspoon sugar**
- **2 tablespoons lemon juice**
- **¼ cup red wine vinegar**
- **1 cup olive or vegetable oil**

1. Combine egg, mustard, onion, salt, pepper, garlic, sugar, lemon juice and vinegar in the container of an electric blender. Cover. Whirl until smooth.
2. Add oil slowly through center of blender cover while blender is running. Dressing will be quite thick. Refrigerate at least 1 hour to blend flavors.

SUNSET SALAD

A dessert salad that's good with a soup and sandwich for lunch.

Makes 8 servings.

- **2 envelopes unflavored gelatin**

¼ cup sugar
½ teaspoon salt
1 can (20 ounces) crushed pineapple in pineapple juice, drained (reserve juice)
½ cup water
1 cup orange juice
¼ cup cider vinegar
1½ cups shredded carrots (about 3)
Fruit Dressing (recipe follows)

1. Mix gelatin, sugar and salt in a small saucepan; stir in reserved juice from pineapple and water. Heat slowly, stirring constantly, until gelatin dissolves; stir in orange juice and vinegar; pour into a large bowl.
2. Refrigerate until mixture is as thick as unbeaten egg white, about 1 hour.
3. Stir in crushed pineapple and carrots; pour into 6-cup mold or 8 × 8 × 2-inch pan. Refrigerate until firm. Serve with Fruit Dressing.
Fruit Dressing: Combine 1 cup dairy sour cream, 1 teaspoon grated orange rind and 2 tablespoons honey in a small bowl. Beat until smooth; chill. Makes about 1 cup.

MOLDED SPICED FRUIT SALAD

All the delicious flavor of spiced peaches in a colorful fruit gelatin mold.

Makes 6 servings.

1 can (16 ounces) cling peach slices
1 package (3 ounces) lemon-flavored gelatin
1 tablespoon sugar
⅛ teaspoon ground cinnamon
⅛ teaspoon ground cloves
¾ cup boiling water
1 tablespoon vinegar
1 small apple, halved, cored and finely chopped
1½ teaspoons lemon juice
¼ cup finely chopped celery

1. Drain syrup from peaches into a 2-cup glass measure; reserve. Finely chop peaches.
2. Combine gelatin, sugar, cinnamon and cloves in a medium-size bowl; add boiling water, stirring until gelatin and sugar dissolve. Stir in reserved peach syrup (¾ cup) and vine-gar. Chill for 30 minutes or until as thick as unbeaten egg white.
3. Toss apple with lemon juice in a small bowl; fold apple, celery and chopped peaches into gelatin mixture; spoon into a 4-cup mold, an 8 × 8 × 2-inch pan or individual custard cups. Chill until firm.
4. Unmold. Serve on lettuce leaves topped with mayonnaise or creamy salad dressing, if you wish.

RAW MUSHROOM VINAIGRETTE

Makes about 6 servings.

1 pound mushrooms, thinly sliced
½ cup sliced green onions
½ cup chopped fresh parsley
⅓ cup olive or vegetable oil
3 tablespoons lemon juice
1 teaspoon leaf basil, crumbled
1 teaspoon salt
¼ teaspoon pepper

1. Place mushrooms, green onions and parsley in a bowl.
2. Combine oil, lemon juice, basil, salt and pepper in a small jar with a tight-fitting lid; cover; shake. Pour over mushrooms; toss gently. Cover with plastic wrap; refrigerate 2 hours or longer.

MID-EASTERN TABBOULEH SALAD

Makes 4 to 6 servings.

1½ cups boiling water
2 beef bouillon cubes
1 cup bulgur (dried, cooked cracked wheat)
¼ cup chopped green onions with green tops
1 cup chopped fresh parsley
¼ cup chopped fresh mint
3 tomatoes, peeled and chopped (2 cups)
⅓ cup olive oil
¼ cup lemon juice
1 teaspoon salt
⅛ teaspoon pepper
Romaine leaves

1. Pour boiling water over bouillon cubes in a 2-cup measure. Stir to dissolve. Pour over bulgur in large bowl. Let stand until liquid is absorbed.
2. Stir in onions, parsley, mint and tomatoes. Stir oil, lemon juice, salt and pepper in a 1-cup measure until blended. Pour over bulgur mixture; mix well.
3. Cover and chill several hours or overnight. Serve in a romaine-lined salad bowl.

GRAPE AND ENDIVE SALAD

Makes 12 servings.

3 tablespoons lemon juice
¼ cup olive oil
1 tablespoon honey
¼ teaspoon ground cardamom
Dash salt
3 cups seedless green or red grapes
1 cup sliced celery
2 heads Belgian endive, sliced
Celery leaves and grapes for garnish

Mix lemon juice, oil, honey, cardamom and salt in a large bowl; toss in grapes and celery. Chill about 1 hour; toss in endive. Garnish with crisp celery leaves and a cluster of grapes.

GERMAN POTATO SALAD

Makes 6 servings.

6 medium-size potatoes (about 2 pounds)
6 bacon slices
1 medium-size onion, chopped (½ cup)
1 cup chopped celery
1½ tablespoons flour
2 tablespoons sugar
1 teaspoon salt
¼ teaspoon pepper
¼ cup cider vinegar
1 cup water

1. Cook potatoes in boiling water to cover in a large saucepan just until tender, about 20 minutes. Drain; peel and slice into a large bowl; cover.
2. Cook bacon in a large skillet until crisp; drain on paper toweling. Pour off drippings; measure ¼ cup and return to skillet.
3. Sauté onion and celery in drippings until soft. Stir in flour, sugar, salt, pepper, vinegar and water. Cook, stirring constantly, until mixture is thickened. Pour over potatoes; toss lightly to coat. Crumble bacon and sprinkle over top. Serve warm.

FROZEN FRUIT SALAD

Makes 12 servings.

- **5 ripe bananas**
- **1 can (20 ounces) crushed pineapple, drained**
- **1½ cups sugar**
- **¼ cup lemon juice**
- **1 jar (8 ounces) maraschino cherries, chopped (about ⅔ cup; reserve juice)**
- **2 containers (16 ounces each) dairy sour cream**
- **1 can (6 ounces) pecans, chopped (about 1⅔ cups)**

1. Mash bananas in a large bowl. Add drained pineapple, sugar, lemon juice, chopped cherries and their juice. Stir until blended.
2. Fold in sour cream and chopped pecans. Blend well. Turn mixture into a 10-cup ring mold. Cover with aluminum foil. Freeze 8 hours or until firm; unmold.

CUCUMBER SALAD À LA CREME

Fresh mint gives this salad a cool and refreshing taste.

Makes 8 servings.

- **4 to 5 cucumbers (about 2¼ pounds)**
- **1 teaspoon salt**
- **5 tablespoons olive or vegetable oil**
- **1 tablespoon white vinegar**
- **1 tablespoon lemon juice**
- **1 teaspoon Dijon mustard**
- **¼ teaspoon freshly ground pepper**
- **½ cup dairy sour cream**
- **2 tablespoons finely chopped mint**
- **2 tablespoons finely chopped chives or fresh parsley**

1. Score cucumber skins with tines of fork. Cut in half lengthwise. Remove the seeds with tip of a teaspoon. Cut cucumber into ⅛-inch slices; place in a colander. Sprinkle with salt. Stir to mix and let stand 30 minutes.
2. Rinse cucumbers well under running cold water; pat dry on paper toweling.
3. Beat olive oil, vinegar, lemon juice, mustard and pepper in a large bowl with whisk or fork. Add sour cream, mint and chives. Add the well-dried cucumbers; toss lightly. Taste for additional salt. Chill at least 4 hours.

MACARONI SHELL SALAD

Macaroni shells elegantly dressed with sour cream and light cream. You can vary the pasta, if you like, but the flavor is still delightful.

Makes 12 servings.

- **1 package (1 pound) small shell macaroni**
- **1 cup mayonnaise or salad dressing**
- **1 container (8 ounces) dairy sour cream**
- **¾ cup light cream or half-and-half**
- **2 teaspoons salt**
- **½ teaspoon pepper**
- **2 cups sliced celery**
- **1 medium-size green pepper, seeded and diced (1 cup)**
- **1 medium-size red onion, chopped (½ cup)**

1. Cook macaroni following label directions; drain. Rinse with cold water. Drain well.
2. Mix mayonnaise, sour cream, light cream, salt and pepper in a large bowl until smooth.
3. Add macaroni, celery, green pepper and red onion to mixture. Toss gently to coat with dressing. Chill 2 to 3 hours.

CREAMY COLESLAW

Some like coleslaw with oil and vinegar, others with boiled dressing. Here is a tart-sweet variation that's sure to be a hit.

Makes about 8 cups.

- **1 large head cabbage (about 4 pounds), shredded**
- **¼ cup sugar**
- **¼ cup lemon juice**
- **¾ cup mayonnaise or salad dressing**
- **½ teaspoon salt**
- **¼ teaspoon pepper**
- **1 cup grated carrots**
- **½ cup diced green pepper**

1. Place shredded cabbage in a very large bowl; sprinkle with sugar; toss just until mixed; cover. Chill 30 minutes.
2. Mix lemon juice and mayonnaise in a small bowl; pour over cabbage. Sprinkle with salt and pepper; add carrots and green pepper; toss to mix well.

FRESH FRUIT SALAD WITH ORANGE-YOGURT DRESSING

Makes 8 servings.

- **Romaine leaves**
- **2 navel oranges, pared and sectioned**
- **2 grapefruit, pared and sectioned**
- **2 large avocados**
- **Lemon juice**
- **2 large fresh pears**
- **⅓ cup chopped macadamia nuts or walnuts**
- **Watercress**
- **Orange-Yogurt Dressing (recipe follows)**

1. Line serving platter with crisp, chilled romaine leaves. Arrange orange and grapefruit sections alternately in spoke fashion.
2. Peel and pit avocados; slice; sprinkle with lemon juice. Core pears from bottom, keeping pears whole. Cut into crosswise slices. Brush each with lemon juice. Arrange on platter.
3. Sprinkle chopped nuts over arranged fruits. Garnish with watercress. Serve with Orange-Yogurt Dressing.

ORANGE-YOGURT DRESSING

Makes about 2 cups.

- **½ cup sugar**
- **1 tablespoon cornstarch**
- **¼ teaspoon salt**
- **1 teaspoon grated orange rind**
- **1 cup orange juice**
- **2 eggs, beaten**
- **1 container (8 ounces) plain yogurt**

1. Combine sugar, cornstarch and salt in small saucepan. Stir in orange rind and juice. Cook over medium heat, stirring constantly, until thickened and clear.
2. Stir about ¼ cup of juice mixture slowly into beaten eggs in a small bowl. Return to saucepan. Cook about 1 minute longer. Refrigerate until thoroughly cold. Fold in yogurt. Refrigerate.

Pictured opposite: Bean Sprouts and Tomato Salad, page 590

Salad

GREEN BEAN AND MUSHROOM SALAD

Makes 6 servings.

- **1 tablespoon wine vinegar**
- **3 tablespoons olive or vegetable oil**
- **½ cup minced green onions**
- **1 teaspoon Dijon mustard**
- **½ teaspoon salt**
- **⅛ teaspoon freshly ground pepper**
- **½ pound mushrooms**
- **1 pound green beans**
- **1 container (8 ounces) dairy sour cream**
- **Cherry tomatoes**

1. Combine vinegar, oil, green onions, mustard, salt and pepper in a jar with tight-fitting lid; cover; shake until well mixed.
2. Quarter or slice the mushrooms into a large bowl. Pour the dressing over; toss lightly and let stand.
3. Trim beans; snap to 1-inch lengths. Cook in boiling water in a large saucepan for 8 minutes or until barely tender. Drain; run under cold water to stop further cooking; drain.
4. Combine beans and sour cream with marinated mushrooms; toss lightly. Refrigerate; remove salad from refrigerator about 20 minutes before serving. Taste; add additional seasoning, if necessary. Garnish with cherry tomatoes.

— ●●● —

SALAD DRESSING A dressing, whether based on mayonnaise, oil, vinegar, lemon juice or yogurt, will enhance any salad. Use only enough dressing to moisten a salad and bring out all the superb flavor, not to drown it. In most cases, a dressing should be added just before serving.

GREEN GODDESS DRESSING

Makes 1½ cups.

- **1 cup mayonnaise**
- **1 can (2 ounces) flat anchovy fillets, drained**
- **¼ cup chopped green onions**
- **¼ cup chopped fresh parsley**
- **2 tablespoons tarragon-flavored vinegar**

Combine all ingredients in the container of an electric blender; cover; whirl until smooth, scraping down sides of blender as necessary. Refrigerate 1 hour before serving.

SESAME OIL DRESSING

Makes about 2 cups.

- **½ cup corn oil**
- **½ cup sesame oil**
- **½ cup red wine vinegar**
- **2 tablespoons instant minced onion**
- **1 tablespoon leaf basil, crumbled**
- **1 tablespoon garlic powder**
- **1½ teaspoons salt**
- **1½ teaspoons pepper**
- **1½ teaspoons sugar**
- **1½ teaspoons celery seeds**
- **1 teaspoon paprika**
- **1 teaspoon fines herbes**
  - OR: **¼ teaspoon each of parsley, chives, chervil and tarragon**
- **1½ teaspoons bottled liquid seasoning for meats**

Combine ingredients in a jar with a tight-fitting lid. Cover; shake well.

LOW-CALORIE THOUSAND ISLAND DRESSING

Makes 1½ cups.

- **2 tablespoons finely chopped green pepper**
- **1 tablespoon finely chopped celery**
- **1 tablespoon finely chopped canned pimiento**
- **¾ cup chili sauce**
- **1 cup low-calorie mayonnaise**

Combine all ingredients; mix well.

YOGURT DRESSING

Makes about 1 cup.

- **1 container (8 ounces) plain yogurt**
- **1 teaspoon lemon juice**
- **¾ teaspoon salt**
- **¾ teaspoon minced chives**
- **½ teaspoon dry mustard**
- **¼ teaspoon paprika**
- **1 clove garlic, crushed**
- **Freshly ground pepper**

Combine all ingredients in small bowl; cover; refrigerate until serving time.

PROVENCAL TOMATO DRESSING

Makes about 2 cups.

- **1 cup tomato juice**
- **¼ cup olive or vegetable oil**
- **3 tablespoons wine vinegar**
- **2 cloves garlic, crushed**
- **1 teaspoon anchovy paste**
- **½ teaspoon dry mustard**
- **1 teaspoon leaf basil or oregano, crumbled**
- **2 tablespoons chopped fresh parsley**
- **½ teaspoon salt**
- **¼ teaspoon pepper**

Combine tomato juice, oil, vinegar, garlic, anchovy paste, mustard, basil, parsley, salt and pepper in a medium-size jar with a tight-fitting lid; cover; shake. Refrigerate; shake again before using.

PESTO DRESSING

This lively dressing for garden salads can also serve as a wonderful dip for fresh vegetables.

Makes 1 cup.

- **½ cup olive or vegetable oil**
- **¼ cup tarragon-flavored vinegar**
- **1 cup parsley sprigs***
- **1½ teaspoons leaf basil***
- **1 clove garlic**
- **½ teaspoon salt**
- **⅛ teaspoon pepper**
- **2 tablespoons grated Parmesan cheese**

Combine oil, vinegar, parsley, basil, garlic, salt and pepper in the container of an electric blender. Cover. Whirl on high speed until smooth. Stir in cheese. Chill 1 hour for flavors to blend.

If you have fresh basil, substitute 1 cup of basil leaves, loosely packed, for the parsley and dried leaf basil, if you wish.

LEMON FRENCH DRESSING

Makes 1⅓ cups.

- **1 cup olive or vegetable oil**
- **⅓ cup lemon juice**
- **½ teaspoon dry mustard**
- **½ teaspoon paprika**
- **1 teaspoon sugar**
- **1 teaspoon salt**
- **¼ teaspoon pepper**

2 tablespoons finely snipped
fresh herbs (basil, dill,
marjoram, oregano, thyme)
OR: 2 teaspoons dried herbs (½
teaspoon basil, ½ teaspoon
marjoram, ½ teaspoon
oregano, ½ teaspoon thyme)

Combine oil, lemon juice, mustard, paprika, sugar, salt and pepper in a medium-size jar with a tight-fitting lid; cover; shake. Add herbs; shake again. Refrigerate; shake again before using.

———— ●●● ————

SALAMI A sausage of Italian origin, though many countries including the United States produce salamis. The word salami is based on an Italian word meaning "salted," which describes a long-standing method of preserving meat.

Salamis differ in the kinds of meat used, the salting and curing process and their shape. A salami may contain pork and beef or only one type of meat. The meat can be finely ground or coarsely ground with a lot of fat added. Generally you will find two types of salami—soft and hard. Soft salami is made from a coarsely ground mixture of cured beef and pork which is cooked, then air-dried for a short period of time. Whole peppercorns may be mixed into the large links to give it a distinctive appearance. Two favorite soft salamis are *cotto* and *beer* salami. Cotto salami, which literally means "cooked sausage," is mild-flavored and contains peppercorns. Beer salami is garlic-flavored without peppercorns. The hard salamis are highly seasoned with garlic; some are lightly smoked and all are air-dried to make them hard. *Genoa* and *pepperoni* are two favorite hard salamis. Hard salamis are usually sliced wafer-thin and eaten cold in salad or appetizer platters and sandwiches. They may be added to pizzas or pastas.

PEPPERONI PEPPER PIZZAS

Bake at 450° for 10 minutes.
Makes 8 servings as a snack, 4 as a main dish.

Tomato Sauce (*recipe follows*)
1 medium-size green pepper,
halved, seeded and cut into
strips
2 tablespoons olive or vegetable
oil
8 ounces pepperoni, thinly sliced
2 pita breads (about 5 to 6 inches
in diameter), split to make 4
circles
6 ounces mozzarella cheese,
thinly sliced

1. Prepare Tomato Sauce.
2. Sauté pepper in oil in a small skillet, stirring frequently, about 3 minutes or until tender. Remove from skillet; drain. Preheat oven to 450°.
3. Add the pepperoni to the skillet and sauté slightly until browned. Remove from skillet; drain.
4. Place pita circles, rough-sides up, slightly apart on large ungreased baking pan. Spread with Tomato Sauce, then pepperoni slices, cheese and green pepper, dividing equally.
5. Bake in a preheated very hot oven (450°) for 10 minutes or until cheese is melted and lightly browned. Cut into wedges.

TOMATO SAUCE

Makes enough sauce for 4 pitas.

1 medium-size onion, finely
chopped (½ cup)
2 large cloves garlic, finely
chopped
2 tablespoons olive or vegetable
oil
1 can (16 ounces) tomatoes,
drained and chopped
¼ cup tomato paste
1½ teaspoons leaf thyme or basil,
crumbled
1 teaspoon leaf oregano,
crumbled
¼ teaspoon salt
Dash cayenne

1. Sauté onion and garlic in oil in a small skillet, stirring occasionally, 3 minutes or until tender.
2. Add tomatoes, tomato paste, thyme, oregano, salt and cayenne. Cook, uncovered, stirring occasionally, 10 minutes or until thickened.

———— ●●● ————

SALLY LUNN A yeast-leavened bun baked in a Turk's-head mold which originated in England during the 1700's. According to legend, the buns were invented and sold by a girl named Sally Lunn in Bath, England.

SALMON Known and valued by man some 10 to 15 thousand years ago, salmon is still a prized food. When the Romans saw the salmon for the first time about 56 B.C. they called the fish the leaper or "salmo." Salmon soon found its way to the banquet tables. In the 17th century, salt salmon was an important item of trade between Scotland and England. In America, the Northwest Indians worshiped salmon, believing the fish was sent by the Indian gods. They smoked and dried salmon for winter use. They also dried and pounded salmon to a powder and used it as an item of trade with the Plains Indians. Through the ages, salmon has been served as food fit for kings.

Salmon was once an abundant fish of the Northern Hemisphere. The encroachment of civilization and overfishing have reduced the number of salmon. World-wide conservation measures are now protecting the salmon supply.

A salmon spends most of its life in salt water; the length of time spent in fresh water varies with the different species. Some salmon go to the ocean only a few days after hatching in rivers and streams, while others remain in fresh water up to 2 to 3 years. In the spring and fall, mature salmon begin their journey back to their spawning grounds. It is at this time that the majority of the salmon are caught.

Only one species of salmon lives in the Atlantic Ocean. A few Atlantic salmon may be found in the rivers of Maine, but most are caught off the coasts of Canada and Europe. There are five salmon species in the Pacific Ocean: sockeye, chinook, coho, pink and chum.

Sockeye salmon is also called "red sockeye" or "blueback." It is the most valuable species for canning. Seldom

Salmon

marketed fresh, the sockeye has a deep red flesh and weighs about 7 pounds. It is caught off Alaska, in the Puget Sound and in the Columbia River.

Chinook is the largest of the salmon, averaging 22 pounds in weight. It is also known as "king" or "spring" salmon. Fished from the Columbia River, the chinook has a softer texture than the other species. The color of its flesh ranges from deep red to white.

The coho or silver salmon averages about 8 pounds. Its red flesh is lighter than that of the sockeye. Pink salmon is the smallest of all the salmon, averaging about 4½ pounds in weight. The flesh is a light peach color. This species accounts for nearly half the salmon that is canned. Chum or keta salmon is the least expensive of all canned salmon. The flesh is not red, but slightly gray. It has less oil content than the other species. The chum is also smoked. Although the flesh is less desirable than the other species, the roe from the female is prized for caviar.

Salmon is considered a fat fish, its flesh containing large amounts of natural oil. It is best when cooked simply. Salmon is a high quality protein food, rich in phosphorus, potassium, niacin, riboflavin and some vitamin A. Fresh salmon steak, about 6¾ × 2½ × 1-inches, broiled with butter has 145 calories. A 3½-ounce serving of canned pink salmon has 141 calories; red salmon contains 171 calories. One ounce of smoked salmon contains 50 calories.

Buying and Storing: Salmon is marketed fresh, smoked, canned and frozen. Fresh salmon is sold whole, as steaks, fillets or large pieces.

Smoked salmon is sold under names such as "Nova," "Scotch" and "lox." European smoked Scotch salmon is made from the Atlantic salmon. Nova salmon may have originated in Nova Scotia, but the term applies to Pacific salmon smoked in New York City. Originally lox was the mild-cured sides of the Atlantic salmon made popular by the Jewish in London in the late 1800's and intro-duced to America at the turn of the century. Nowadays, lox is made from the chinook salmon, cured in a salt-sugar brine and cold-smoked. European salmon has a heavier smoked taste than American smoked salmon. Generally, the salt content of smoked salmon will vary from processor to processor.

Canned salmon is packed mainly in three sizes. The 15½-ounce can contains 2 cups and serves 4; the 7¾-ounce can contains 1 cup and serves 2; the 3¾-ounce can serves one. All five Pacific salmon species are canned. Sockeye has the firmest texture and darkest red color. Since it is the most expensive salmon canned, use it for appetizers, main dishes and salads where the appearance is important. Use the least expensive chum for casseroles and other cooked dishes where color is not of prime importance.

Frozen salmon is sold whole or cut into steaks. Allow one steak or ½ pound pan-dressed fish per serving. Allow 1 pound of whole or drawn salmon per serving.

The Atlantic salmon, raised on "farms" in Norway, may one day provide fresh salmon to more markets. Presently, farm-fresh salmon is limited to major cities where it is air-freight delivered.

Store fresh salmon in the coldest part of the refrigerator; use within 2 days. Or, wrap for freezing and freeze for longer storage.

SALMON MOUSSE

Gently ease aluminum cups away from mousse for super-easy un-molding.

Makes 6 servings.

- 2 **envelopes unflavored gelatin**
- ⅓ **cup water**
- 2 **tablespoons lemon juice**
- 1 **cup boiling water**
- 1 **can (15½ ounces) pink or red salmon, drained, boned and skinned**
- ½ **cup heavy cream**
- ½ **cup mayonnaise or salad dressing**
- 1 **tablespoon thinly sliced green onion**
- 1 **teaspoon dillweed**
- ½ **teaspoon salt**
- ½ **teaspoon paprika**
- ¼ **teaspoon pepper**
  Marinated Cucumber Slices (recipe follows)
  Lemon slices

1. Sprinkle gelatin over water and lemon juice in container of electric blender; let stand 5 minutes. Add boiling water; cover; whirl for 30 seconds or until smooth.
2. Add salmon, heavy cream, mayonnaise, green onion, dillweed, salt, paprika and pepper. Whirl for 1 minute more or until completely smooth.
3. Pour salmon mixture into 6 reusable aluminum 2⅞ × 1¼-inch cup-cake cups (about ⅔ cup). Chill, covered with aluminum foil, for 3 hours or until set.
4. Gently ease aluminum cups away from salmon mixture, loosening sides with small spatula. Unmold onto serving platter or individual serving plates. Serve with Marinated Cucumber Slices and garnish with slices of lemon.

MARINATED CUCUMBER SLICES

A pretty and tangy-tasting accompaniment to Salmon Mousse.
Makes 6 servings.

- 2 **small or 1 large cucumber, unpeeled, halved lengthwise, seeded and very thinly sliced**
- 1½ **teaspoons salt**
- ½ **cup white wine vinegar**
- ¼ **cup finely chopped fresh parsley**
- ½ **teaspoon sugar**
- ¼ **teaspoon white pepper**

1. Layer cucumber slices with 1 teaspoon of the salt in a 9-inch pie plate. Let stand for 10 minutes.
2. Press cucumbers into plate and pour off liquid that accumulates.
3. Sprinkle vinegar, parsley, sugar, pepper and remaining salt over cucumbers, tossing gently to mix.
4. Marinate, covered, for at least 30 minutes to let flavors blend before serving.

Pictured opposite: Flounder and Salmon Roulade, page 598

Salmon

FLOUNDER AND SALMON ROULADE

Makes 8 servings.

- 1 fresh or thawed, frozen salmon steak (about 1 pound)
- 4 fresh or thawed frozen fillets of flounder or sole fillets (about 8 ounces each)
- 2 teaspoons lemon juice
- ¼ teaspoon pepper
- ½ cup water
- ½ cup dry white wine
- 2 shallots, thinly sliced
- ½ teaspoon salt
- 1 teaspoon leaf tarragon
  Lobster or Crab Sauce (recipe follows)
  Fresh dill sprigs

1. Skin and bone salmon; halve crosswise; cut each half into 4 strips.
2. Halve each flounder fillet lengthwise; sprinkle with lemon juice and pepper. Place a strip of salmon on each fillet. Roll up; secure with wooden picks.
3. Combine water, wine, shallots and salt in a large skillet. Tie tarragon in a small piece of cheesecloth; drop into skillet. Stand fish rolls in skillet.
4. Heat to boiling; lower heat; cover; simmer 5 minutes or until fish loses its translucency, becomes white and feels firm. Remove to a platter; keep warm. Cook pan liquid rapidly until reduced to ½ cup; reserve.
5. Prepare Lobster or Crab Sauce; spoon over fish; garnish with dill.

Lobster or Crab Sauce: Cook 1½ cups heavy cream rapidly in a large saucepan until reduced to 1 cup. Add reserved fish liquid, ¼ teaspoon salt, ⅛ teaspoon paprika and 1 can (6½ ounces) drained, boned and coarsely shredded lobster or crab meat. Heat, stirring until hot.

SAVORY SALMON-STUFFED TOMATOES

Makes about 24 appetizers.

- 1 pint cherry tomatoes
- 1 can (7¾ ounces) red salmon
- ¼ cup dairy sour cream
- 2 tablespoons grated onion
- 2 tablespoons finely chopped fresh parsley
- 1 tablespoon chili sauce
- 2 teaspoons fresh lemon juice
- 1 teaspoon prepared horseradish
- ¼ teaspoon salt

1. Cut tops off cherry tomatoes; scoop out pulp. Drain tomatoes upside down on paper toweling while preparing filling.
2. Drain and flake salmon, removing bones and skin.
3. Combine salmon, sour cream, onion, parsley, chili sauce, lemon juice, horseradish and salt in bowl; mix well.
4. Fill cherry tomatoes with mixture. Chill until serving time. Garnish with parsley, if you wish.

DILLED SALMON-TOPPED CUCUMBER ROUNDS

Makes about 36 rounds.

- 1 can (7¾ ounces) red salmon, drained and flaked
- 1 package (8 ounces) cream cheese, softened
- 2 teaspoons dillweed
- 1 teaspoon grated lemon rind
- 1 teaspoon lemon juice
- 1 teaspoon minced onion
- 2 cucumbers (each about 10 inches long), unpared

1. Combine drained salmon, cream cheese, dillweed, lemon rind and juice and minced onion in a medium-size bowl. Beat on medium speed with electric mixer until well blended. Refrigerate until stiff enough to pipe onto cucumber rounds.
2. While mixture is chilling, score cucumbers with the tines of a fork. Cut each into eighteen ¼-inch slices. Fit a star tip onto a pastry bag; fill with salmon mixture; pipe onto cucumber rounds. Garnish with dill.

SMOKED SALMON AND CHEESE CANAPÉS

Makes about 30 canapés.

- 1 package (8 ounces) cream cheese
- ¼ pound sliced smoked salmon
- 1 tablespoon lemon juice
- ¼ cup chopped fresh dill
  Pumpernickel bread
  Red or black lumpfish caviar
  Fresh dill sprigs

1. Soften cream cheese and spread on wax paper to an 8- or 9-inch square. Chop salmon finely; spread evenly over cream cheese, pressing down slightly. Sprinkle with lemon juice. Roll up, jelly-roll fashion, scraping cheese from paper with small spatula as you roll. Roll in chopped dill. Wrap in foil. Chill several hours or until firm enough to slice.
2. To serve: Slice with a thin-bladed sharp knife into about ¼-inch-thick rounds. Arrange on thin slices of party pumpernickel bread. Garnish each with caviar and a small sprig of dill.

DOUBLE SALMON CUCUMBERS

Makes about 16 appetizers.

- 1 package (3 ounces) cream cheese, softened
- 2 tablespoons dairy sour cream
- 1 can (3¾ ounces) salmon, drained, boned and skinned
- 3 ounces smoked salmon, chopped
- 2 slices white bread, toasted and crumbled
- ¼ cup thinly sliced green onions
- 2 tablespoons chopped fresh dill
  OR: 2 teaspoons dillweed
- 1 tablespoon lemon juice
- ¼ teaspoon pepper
- 2 large cucumbers, peeled, halved lengthwise and seeded
  Fresh dill sprigs (optional)

1. Combine all ingredients except cucumbers and dill sprigs in a small bowl and blend thoroughly.
2. Mound the filling into each cucumber half. Place on double thickness of paper toweling and wrap tightly in plastic wrap. Refrigerate several hours or overnight.
3. About 1 hour before serving, cut filled cucumber into 1½-inch lengths and arrange on a serving plate. Garnish with dill sprigs, if you wish. Cover and refrigerate until just before serving.

COULIBIAC SALAD

Makes 8 servings.

- 1½ cups uncooked long-grain rice
- 1 can (4 ounces) sliced mushrooms, drained

½ cup snipped fresh dill
¾ cup mayonnaise
¼ cup dry white wine
1 teaspoon salt
　Few grains pepper
2 cans (15½ ounces each) salmon, drained, boned and broken up
1 cup thinly sliced celery
6 tablespoons vegetable oil
2 tablespoons lemon juice
1 teaspoon salt
　Pinch pepper
2 tomatoes, cut in thin wedges
　Thin lemon slices, halved

1. Cook rice following label directions; cool to room temperature. Stir in mushrooms and dill; chill.
2. Combine mayonnaise, wine, 1 teaspoon salt and pepper in a small bowl; mix well. Mix gently into rice. Press rice mixture into a 6-cup ring mold. Cover and refrigerate about 2 hours or until thoroughly chilled.
3. Combine salmon and celery in a medium-size bowl. Beat oil with lemon juice and remaining salt and pepper in a cup. Pour over salmon mixture; stir gently to mix. Cover; refrigerate until serving time.
4. Just before serving, unmold rice ring onto serving platter; spoon salmon mixture into center. Arrange tomato wedges around rice ring. Tuck lemon slices between rice and salmon mixture.

ORANGE SALMON PATTIES

Makes 4 servings.

1 small orange
1 can (15½ ounces) salmon
1 medium-size onion, minced (½ cup)
1 egg
1 cup packaged bread crumbs
¾ teaspoon salt
¼ teaspoon pepper
¼ cup vegetable oil
¼ cup mayonnaise or salad dressing
¼ cup plain yogurt
2 tablespoons orange juice

1. Pare skin from orange (no white); section, seed and cut orange into small pieces; place in large bowl.
2. Remove bones and skin from sal-mon and flake into bowl with orange pieces; add onion, egg, bread crumbs, salt and pepper; mix lightly. (It's quickest with your hands.) Shape into 8 patties.
3. Sauté patties in hot oil in a large skillet until golden brown, turning once.
4. Combine mayonnaise, yogurt and orange juice in a small bowl; serve with patties.

BAKED SALMON AND GREEN BEAN PUFF

Bake at 375° for 50 minutes.
Makes 4 servings.

1 package (9 ounces) frozen cut green beans
2 tablespoons water
1 can (15½ ounces) salmon
1 can condensed Cheddar cheese soup
2 tablespoons flour
1 tablespoon grated Parmesan cheese
½ teaspoon dillweed
1 tablespoon prepared spicy brown mustard
1 tablespoon minced drained capers
1 tablespoon caper juice
⅛ teaspoon pepper
Soufflé Topping:
4 eggs, separated
¼ teaspoon salt
¼ teaspoon dillweed
　Pinch pepper
2 tablespoons grated Parmesan cheese

1. Cook beans in water in a small covered saucepan over moderate heat, about 5 minutes until tender but still crisp.
2. Meanwhile, drain and flake the salmon, discarding any large bones or pieces of skin. Blend ¼ cup of the soup with the flour, then combine with the remaining soup; mix in grated Parmesan, dillweed, mustard, minced capers, caper juice and pepper.
3. Drain beans well and place in an 8-cup soufflé dish. Add salmon and cheese soup mixture; stir well to mix. Bake, uncovered, in a moderate oven (375°) for 20 minutes.

4. When casserole has baked almost 20 minutes, prepare Soufflé Topping. Beat egg whites with salt to soft peaks; beat yolks with dillweed and pepper until smooth, then stir in grated Parmesan. Spoon a little beaten whites into yolk mixture, then pour yolks over whites and fold in gently until no streaks of white or yellow show. Spoon quickly on top of hot beans and salmon, return to oven and bake 30 minutes longer until puffy and touched with brown. Serve immediately.

BAKED SALMON WITH SOUR CREAM DILL SAUCE

Bake at 375° for about 1 hour.
Makes 8 servings.

1 center-cut fresh salmon steak (3½ to 4 pounds)
2 tablespoons chopped shallots
2 stalks fresh dill
¼ cup dry white wine
½ teaspoon leaf tarragon, crumbled,
　OR: 6 sprigs fresh tarragon
1 teaspoon salt
　Sour Cream Dill Sauce (recipe follows)

1. Preheat oven to 375°. Rinse fish in cold water; pat dry with paper toweling. Tear off piece of heavy-duty aluminum foil large enough to enclose fish. Place fish in center of foil; fold up sides. Place 1 tablespoon of the shallots and 1 stalk of the dill on fish.
2. Combine wine, tarragon, salt, remaining shallots and dill in a small saucepan. Simmer until reduced by half; pour over the fish. Close the foil tightly. Place fish packet in a baking pan.
3. Bake in a preheated oven (375°) for 20 to 25 minutes per pound. Serve with Sour Cream Dill Sauce.

SOUR CREAM DILL SAUCE:

Combine 1 cup dairy sour cream, ¼ cup mayonnaise, 2 tablespoons chopped fresh dill, 1 tablespoon drained capers, 1 teaspoon lemon juice, ½ teaspoon salt and ¼ teaspoon freshly ground pepper in a small bowl. Refrigerate until serving time. Makes 1¼ cups.

●●●

Salt

SALT A condiment or food flavoring, salt has been used for centuries as a food preservative. Because salt had the power to preserve food, a country without salt could starve. In Roman times, salt was such a valuable commodity that it was given to soldiers as compensation for services. This salt money or *salarium* is the origin of *salary* today. Cakes of salt were exchanged like money.

Chemically known as sodium chloride, salt occurs abundantly in seas and some lakes in addition to crystalline deposits in the earth. It is obtained by allowing the water from seas or salty lakes to evaporate naturally in shallow pools or man-made heated pans. It is also obtained from underground deposits which were made from the evaporation of prehistoric seas. It is mined like coal or dissolved with water and the brine is pumped to the surface and evaporated. Salt is then refined and packaged for the marketplace.

Buying Salt: *Table* or *common salt* is fine-grained and contains a harmless chemical such as magnesium carbonate or calcium phosphate that prevents the absorption of moisture and keeps the salt free-flowing. It is available plain or iodized. Iodized salt has potassium iodide added and should be used by those who might be deficient in iodine.

Sea salt is obtained by evaporating sea water. Sea salt is coarse-grained with natural iodine and minerals. It does have a slightly different flavor from table salt.

Kosher salt is fine-grained sea salt. It is also called flake, dairy or cheese salt.

Pickling salt is fine-grained pure salt without any additives. It is also called canning salt.

Rock salt is very large grains of unrefined salt. It is used for keeping oysters or clams on the half-shell upright during baking or in ice cream freezers when making ice cream.

Salt is often combined with herbs, spices or other ingredients to form special flavored salts such as *seasoned salt, celery salt* and *garlic salt.*

SANDWICH There's no limit to what a sandwich can be. Just about everyone goes for this easy, quick, portable meal. The sandwich was named for John Montagu, the 4th Earl of Sandwich, a gambler who hated to leave the gaming table. His chef brought him a meal of cold beef slices between bread so that he could eat as he played. Since the Earl's era in the 18th century, the sandwich has been acceptable as a meal. The variety of breads, fillings and toppers available in your supermarket can inspire delicious creations. Here is a round-up of classic and special sandwiches.

SUPER CHEESE HERO
Makes 1 sandwich.

- ½ **small red pepper, seeded and cut into strips**
- ½ **small green pepper, seeded and cut into strips**
- 2 **teaspoons olive oil**
- ⅛ **teaspoon crushed red pepper**
- ⅛ **teaspoon leaf basil, crumbled**
- ⅛ **teaspoon leaf oregano, crumbled**
- 1 **French roll or hero roll**
- 4 **thin slices mozzarella cheese**
- 5 **flat anchovy fillets**

1. Sauté red and green pepper strips in oil in a small skillet until crisp-tender. Sprinkle with red pepper, basil and oregano. Remove from heat.
2. Cut thin slice from the top of roll; scoop out center of roll. Place roll on rack over broiler pan. Broil 4 inches from broiler until lightly browned.
3. Spoon pepper mixture into shell. Top with mozzarella. Broil just to melt cheese. Crisscross anchovy fillets over cheese. Cover filling with top of roll.

PROVENÇAL PAN BAGNA

This appealing French sandwich is ideal for a picnic in the park or at the beach. Also called "pan bagnat" or "pain baigné," the name means "bathed bread" as the bread is bathed in olive oil for flavor.

Makes 4 servings.

- 4 **hard-crusted French rolls or hero rolls**
- ½ **cup olive oil**
- 2 **tablespoons red wine vinegar**
- 2 **cloves garlic, minced**
- ¼ **teaspoon leaf basil, crumbled**
- 2 **medium-size tomatoes, halved and thinly sliced**
- 1 **small green pepper, halved, seeded and cut into thin strips**
- 1 **small red onion, sliced and separated into rings**
  Salt
  Pepper
- 4 **hard-cooked eggs, sliced**
- 1 **can (2 ounces) flat anchovy fillets, drained (12)**
- 10 **pitted ripe olives, halved**

1. Cut rolls in half horizontally. Combine oil, vinegar, garlic and basil in a 1-cup measure; stir until blended. Drizzle 1 tablespoon mixture on each cut side of rolls.
2. Arrange tomato slices on bottom halves of rolls, overlapping to fit; top with green pepper strips and onion rings. Sprinkle with salt and pepper. Arrange egg slices over onion rings; top with anchovy fillets and olives. Sprinkle with more salt and pepper; drizzle with any leftover dressing.
3. Carefully place tops of rolls over filled bottoms; press down gently. The flavor of these sandwiches improves on standing a short while. For picnics, wrap in foil or plastic.

BACON-SPINACH JUNIOR CLUB SANDWICHES

The flavor of this sandwich is reminiscent of the popular sweet-sour spinach salad with chopped egg and bacon bits. Called a "junior club," it consists of two slices of bread rather than the usual three.

Makes 4 servings.

- 12 **bacon slices**
- 4 **eggs**
- 1 **medium-size onion, finely chopped (½ cup)**
- ½ **cup mayonnaise**
- 2 **tablespoons red wine vinegar**
- 1 **tablespoon sugar**
- ½ **teaspoon salt**
  Dash pepper
- 8 **slices firm white bread, toasted**
  Spinach leaves
- 12 **cherry tomatoes**

1. Fry bacon until crisp in large skillet; drain on paper toweling. Remove all but about ¼ cup drippings from pan. Break eggs, 1 at a time, into hot drippings; fry until firm, breaking yolks with a pancake turner, and turning them over. Transfer to warm platter. Remove and discard all but 1 tablespoon of the drippings from pan.

2. Cook onion in remaining drippings until tender. Remove from heat. Stir in mayonnaise, vinegar, sugar, salt and pepper.

3. Spread mayonnaise mixture on each slice of toast. Cover four slices with a layer of spinach leaves, 3 slices bacon, a fried egg and top with more spinach leaves. Cover with remaining slices of toast, mayonnaise-coated-side down. With serrated knife, cut sandwiches into 4 triangles.

4. Alternately spear triangles with cherry tomatoes on 8-inch skewers. Serve on platter garnished with a tomato flower and green onion brushes, if you wish. To make flower garnish, take 2 cherry tomatoes; cut one not quite through into 4 wedges, the other into 6 wedges. Remove pulp. Place the 6-petaled tomato inside the 4-petaled tomato. Cut a ½-inch piece of white green onion at the end into crisscross slashes. Spread end out and place in center of tomato flower. For green onion brushes, use 5-inch onions and cut green part into lengthwise shreds about 1 inch long.

THE REUBEN

Makes 6 servings.

12 slices pumpernickel or rye bread
½ cup bottled Russian or Thousand Island dressing
½ pound thinly sliced corned beef
12 thin slices Swiss cheese
1 cup drained sauerkraut
2 tablespoons Dijon mustard
Softened butter or margarine

1. Spread 6 of the bread slices with Russian dressing. Divide corned beef evenly among the slices. Top each with 2 slices of cheese and about 2 tablespoons sauerkraut.

2. Spread remaining bread slices with mustard, and press, mustard-side down, over sandwiches.

3. Spread outside surfaces with butter. Broil or grill sandwiches slowly until cheese melts and bread browns on both sides.

GREEK GYRO

"Gyro" means round. In Greek or Near Eastern restaurants, this sandwich is made with well-seasoned lamb cooked on a slowly rotating vertical spit. As the outer surface of the meat browns, slivers of flavorful hot lamb are cut off.

Makes 6 servings.

1 pound ground lean leg of lamb
1 cup fresh bread crumbs (2 slices)
2 tablespoons chopped fresh parsley
1 large clove garlic, finely chopped
1 teaspoon salt
1 teaspoon chili powder
½ teaspoon ground cumin
¼ teaspoon fenugreek seeds, finely ground
Dash cayenne
6 pita breads
1 small onion
½ cup dairy sour cream
½ teaspoon dillweed
OR: 1½ teaspoons chopped fresh dill
½ teaspoon salt
2 teaspoons lemon juice
1 medium-size tomato
3 cups shredded lettuce
Lemon
Fresh dill sprigs

1. Combine lamb, bread crumbs, parsley, garlic, the 1 teaspoon salt, chili, cumin, fenugreek and cayenne in a large bowl. Mix very well with spoon or with hands.

2. Shape lamb into a 4 × 6-inch patty about 1 inch thick. Broil, turning once, until well browned on each side, about 15 minutes. Remove lamb from broiler and let rest 10 minutes before slicing. Wrap pita breads in aluminum foil; place in hot oven to warm when lamb is removed.

3. Meanwhile, cut onion from top to bottom into julienne strips. Place in bowl with sour cream, dill, the ½ teaspoon salt and lemon juice; stir until mixed. Slice tomato from top to bottom; cut slices into halves.

4. Cut lamb lengthwise into thin strips. Remove pita from foil; fold each pita in half across the center; fill each with some strips of lamb, shredded lettuce, sliced tomatoes and sour cream-onion mixture. For easier eating, wrap one end of each in plastic wrap and, if you wish, overwrap with napkin. Garnish each sandwich with lemon wedges and fresh dill sprigs, if you wish.

WEST COAST HERO

A hero is an American invention sandwich called by other names in various parts of the country—hoagie, submarine, torpedo or zep. It is called "hero" because of the heroic appetite needed to finish the hearty sandwich. This version is particularly popular on the West Coast.

Makes 6 servings.

2 packages (4 ounces each) alfalfa sprouts
1 cup shredded carrots
1 cup mayonnaise
2 teaspoons sugar
2 teaspoons lemon juice
1½ teaspoons salt
Dash pepper
1 large round loaf sourdough bread, about 9 inches in diameter
1 large avocado, pitted, peeled and sliced
¼ pound thinly sliced hard salami
1 package (8 ounces) sliced provolone cheese

1. Mix sprouts, carrots, mayonnaise, sugar, lemon juice, salt and pepper in a large bowl. Cut off top half of bread; scoop out center, leaving a shell about 1 inch thick. (Use inside for crumbs in another recipe.)

2. Place half of sprout mixture on bottom of bread. Top with half of avocado slices; cover with a layer of salami and cheese, then remaining avocado slices and sprout mixture. Replace top of bread. Cut into wedges to serve.

THE IOWA HARVEST

Makes 4 sandwiches.

- **1 package (4 ounces) alfalfa sprouts**
- **⅓ cup mayonnaise or salad dressing**
- **1 tablespoon prepared spicy brown mustard**
- **8 slices wheat germ or rye bread**
- **¼ cup (½ stick) butter or margarine, softened**
  Spinach leaves
- **1 package (8 ounces) sliced cooked ham**
- **1 package (8 ounces) sliced natural caraway cheese (kuminost spiced cheese)**

1. Place alfalfa sprouts in large strainer; rinse under cold running water; drain well, pressing out excess water. Turn into a medium-size bowl. Mix with mayonnaise and mustard.
2. Spread each of the bread slices with butter. On 4 slices of bread, place in order: spinach leaves, alfalfa mixture, divided evenly, ham and cheese, cut to fit. Top with remaining bread slices, buttered-side down.

CROQUE MONSIEUR

Makes 4 servings.

- **8 slices firm white bread, one to two days old**
- **6 tablespoons butter or margarine, softened**
- **12 thin slices cooked ham**
- **4 thin slices Swiss, Gruyère or Muenster cheese**
- **1 tablespoon flour**
- **½ teaspoon salt**
- **⅛ teaspoon pepper**
  Dash paprika or cayenne
- **1 cup light cream or milk**
- **2 ounces Swiss cheese shredded (½ cup)**
- **3 large eggs**
- **3 tablespoons milk**

1. Trim crusts from bread. Spread one side of 4 of the slices with 2 tablespoons of the butter. Top with 2 slices ham, 1 slice cheese and 1 slice ham. Cover with remaining bread slices.
2. Melt 1 tablespoon butter in a medium-size saucepan; blend in flour, salt, pepper and paprika. Slowly stir in cream. Cook, stirring constantly, until thickened and bubbly. Add cheese and cook until melted. Keep warm over low heat.
3. Beat eggs and milk together in a small bowl just until blended. Pour mixture into a pie plate. Dip sandwiches on both sides.
4. Melt the remaining 3 tablespoons butter in a large skillet. Sauté sandwiches, turning once, until golden brown. Add more butter, if needed. Serve with cheese sauce spooned over.

FRENCH ACCENT

Makes 3 servings.

- **3 tablespoons butter or margarine, softened**
- **1 tablespoon Dijon mustard**
- **3 crescent rolls or croissants, split**
- **3 slices roast beef**
- **¼ cup crumbled blue cheese**
- **1 green onion, chopped**
- **1 egg white, stiffly beaten**

1. Mix butter and mustard in a 1-cup measure; spread on cut surfaces of rolls.
2. Roll up roast beef; place on crescent roll bottoms.
3. Gently fold cheese and green onion into beaten egg white in a small bowl; spread over beef.
4. Broil 3 to 4 inches from heat for 2 minutes or until topping is bubbly.

THE WISCONSIN WOW

Makes 4 sandwiches.

- **1 jar (6 ounces) marinated artichoke hearts**
- **8 slices rye or pumpernickel bread**
- **¼ cup (½ stick) butter or margarine, softened**
  Romaine leaves
- **1 package (8 ounces) sliced Muenster cheese**
- **2 packages (8 ounces each) sliced Braunschweiger (12 slices)**
- **1 large ripe tomato, cut into 8 slices**
- **1 medium-size red onion, cut into 8 slices**

1. Drain marinade from artichokes into a 1-cup measure; reserve. Coarsely chop artichokes.
2. Spread each of the bread slices with butter. Arrange romaine on 4 slices of bread. Top with cheese slices. Divide artichokes evenly over the cheese.
3. Overlap one slice Braunschweiger, one slice tomato and one slice onion; repeat one more time, ending with remaining slices of Braunschweiger to fit bread. Drizzle over reserved artichoke marinade. Top with remaining bread slices, buttered-side down.

THE JERSEY JUMBO

Makes 6 servings.

- **2 tablespoons tarragon-flavored vinegar**
- **2 tablespoons olive or vegetable oil**
- **1 tablespoon drained capers**
- **¼ teaspoon Italian herb seasoning mix, crumbled**
- **1 large loaf sesame-seeded French or Italian bread (about 15 inches long)**
- **1 cup shredded iceberg lettuce**
- **1 package (12 ounces) sliced cotto salami**
- **½ pound sliced mortadella**
- **1 package (8 ounces) sliced Provolone cheese, cut in half**
- **1 small sweet red pepper, halved, seeded and cut into thin strips**
- **1 small green pepper, halved, seeded and cut into thin strips**

1. Combine vinegar, oil, capers and Italian seasoning in a 1-cup measure; stir until blended.
2. Cut slice from top of loaf; reserve. Scoop out center of bottom half. (Reserve bread to make crumbs.)
3. Fill bottom of loaf with shredded lettuce. Stir dressing and drizzle half over lettuce. Fold salami and mortadella in quarters. Arrange salami, mortadella and cheese over lettuce. Top with pepper strips. Drizzle with remaining dressing. Cover with reserved top of loaf. Cut into serving-size portions.

Sangria

SANGRIA A red wine punch of Spanish origin traditionally mixed in a pitcher. A cool and refreshing summer drink, sangria is made by pouring a light red wine into a pitcher with sliced oranges, sliced lemon, a bit of sugar, a splash of brandy or other liqueur, and finally soda water and ice. It is mixed with a wooden spoon and served by the glassful. White wine may also be used for sangria but red wine is the favorite.

SANGRIA

Makes about 3 quarts.

- 2 bottles (750 ml. each) red wine
- 1 cup orange juice
- ¼ cup lime juice
- ⅔ cup sugar
- ½ cup orange-flavored liqueur
- 2 bottles (12 ounces each) club soda, chilled
  Ice cubes
  Orange slices
  Lime slices

1. Combine wine, orange and lime juices and sugar in a very large pitcher or punch bowl; stir until sugar is dissolved; add liqueur; chill.
2. Just before serving, add club soda, ice cubes and orange and lime slices.

SUMMER SANGRIA

Makes about 2 quarts.

- 1 cup sugar
- 1½ cups water
- 1 cup orange juice
- ½ cup brandy
- 1 large orange, sliced and quartered
- 1 lime, sliced
- 1 cup honeydew melon balls
  Ice cubes
- 1 bottle (750 ml.) dry white wine, chilled

1. Combine sugar and water in large pitcher; stir until sugar dissolves. Add orange juice, brandy, orange, lime and honeydew. Chill 2 hours.
2. Just before serving, add ice cubes and stir in chilled wine.

— ●●● —

SANTA CLAUS MELON A large, oval, greenish-gold melon available in December or around Christmastime —hence its name. The flesh is yellow to pale green, similar to honeydew. It is juicy and sweet. When ripe, the melon turns soft at the blossom end and the rind turns yellow. This melon is sometimes called Christmas Melon or Winter Casaba. See also **MELON**.

SARDINE The term "sardine" is not the name of any one fish in the sea, but a word used for a number of small, silvery, soft-boned fish such as herring, pilchard, alewife and sprat. It was probably the pilchard, found in abundance around the island of Sardinia in the Mediterranean Sea, from which the overall name is derived.

Although there are some size, texture and flavor differences among the various fishes canned as sardines, generally they are interchangeable in recipes for appetizers, sandwiches and salads, providing they are packed in a similar sauce or oil. Some are packed in soybean oil, others in olive oil; some in flavored sauces such as tomato or mustard sauce. Sardines are often boned and skinned before being packed. In Maine, small herring are canned as sardines. In some countries, sardines are marketed fresh or lightly salted. In the United States, only canned sardines are readily available.

PORTUGUESE SEAFOOD SALAD

Makes 6 servings.

- ½ package (1 pound size) orzo or rice-shaped pasta (1¼ cups)
- 1 can (4½ ounces) shrimp
- 1 teaspoon finely chopped lemon rind (bright yellow part only)
- ¼ cup lemon juice
- 2 tablespoons finely chopped onion
- ¾ teaspoon salt
- 1 jar (6 ounces) marinated artichoke hearts
- ¼ teaspoon crumbled saffron threads
- 1 tablespoon warm water
- ½ cup cooked frozen green peas
  Lettuce leaves
- 2 cans (about 4 ounces each) sardines
  Lemon slices
  Watercress

1. Cook orzo in boiling water following label directions; drain; rinse with cold water; drain well.
2. Drain shrimp; rinse with cold water; place in large bowl; add lemon rind, lemon juice, onion, salt and artichokes with marinade. Soak saffron in warm water 5 minutes; add to bowl. Add the orzo and peas; toss well to mix. Refrigerate, stirring once or twice, at least 2 hours or until well chilled.
3. To serve: Arrange the orzo mixture on lettuce leaves on a platter. Arrange sardines on top. Garnish with lemon and watercress.

RUSSIAN FISH SALAD PLATTER

Makes 4 servings.

- 1 package (10 ounces) frozen mixed vegetables
- ½ cup mayonnaise
- 1 tablespoon Dijon mustard
- 1 cup diced celery
- 4 hard-cooked eggs, chopped
- 2 tablespoons minced onion
  Salad greens
- 2 cans (7 ounces each) skinless and boneless sardines

1. Cook frozen vegetables following label directions until crisp-tender. Drain, rinse with cold water until vegetables are cold and drain on paper toweling.
2. Blend mayonnaise with mustard in a medium-size bowl. Fold in the vegetables, celery, eggs and onion.
3. Line a serving platter with greens, mound salad in center and surround with whole sardines.

— ●●● —

SAUCE A sauce is used either to enhance the flavor of other foods or to bind foods together. What would spaghetti be without a hearty meat sauce; what would spareribs be without a barbecue sauce? A soufflé or croquette would never hold together without a basic white sauce. The success of many recipes depends upon its sauce. And, a sauce can make a good dish taste even better. See also **BÉCHAMEL, BÉARNAISE, BORDE- LAISE, HARD SAUCE, HOLLAN- DAISE, MORNAY SAUCE, POLO- NAISE SAUCE.**

BASIC WHITE SAUCE

Makes 2 cups.

Thin Sauce:
- 2 tablespoons butter or margarine
- 2 tablespoons flour
- ½ teaspoon salt
- ⅛ teaspoon pepper
- 2 cups milk

Uses: Cream soups, chowders, casseroles, sauces.

Medium Sauce:
- ¼ cup (½ stick) butter or margarine
- ¼ cup all-purpose flour
- ½ teaspoon salt
- ⅛ teaspoon pepper
- 2 cups milk

Uses: Creamed dishes, sauces, gravies.

Thick Sauce:
- 6 tablespoons (¾ stick) butter or margarine
- 6 tablespoons all-purpose flour
- ½ teaspoon salt
- ⅛ teaspoon pepper
- 2 cups milk

Uses: Soufflés, croquettes, patties.

1. Melt butter over *low* heat in medium-size, heavy saucepan. It should just melt—not bubble and turn brown. (Use a wooden spoon or wire whisk for stirring.)
2. Have the flour, salt and pepper measured and ready. Stir quickly into melted butter, then cook, stirring constantly, just until it bubbles.
3. Now stir in the milk *slowly*. (This helps to keep sauce from lumping.) Continue cooking and stirring from bottom of pan until sauce thickens and bubbles 3 minutes.

New Delhi Cream: Blend ½ cup mayonnaise or salad dressing, ½ teaspoon grated onion and ¼ teaspoon curry powder into 1 cup of hot Thin White Sauce. Delicious on green peas. Makes 1½ cups.

Old-Fashioned Cheese Sauce: Stir 1 cup (4 ounces) shredded Cheddar cheese and ¼ teaspoon dry mustard into 1 cup hot Thin White Sauce. Serve the sauce over cauliflower, broccoli or green beans. It's also good over poached fish fillets. Makes 1¼ cups.

Anchovy Sauce: Blend 1 teaspoon anchovy paste into 1 cup hot Thin White Sauce. Serve the sauce over freshly boiled potatoes or green peas. Makes 1 cup.

Spring Egg Sauce: Stir 1 chopped hard-cooked egg, 1 tablespoon cut chives and a dash of seasoned salt into 1 cup hot Medium White Sauce. Serve over cooked, well-drained spinach. Makes 1¼ cups.

Pink Sauce: Stir 2 tablespoons catsup and 2 teaspoons prepared horseradish into 1 cup hot Medium White Sauce. Spoon it over a freshly cooked head of cauliflower. Makes about 1 cup.

SAUSAGE SAUCE

Serve over hot, cooked spaghetti.

Makes 4 cups.

- ½ pound hot or sweet Italian sausages, or a combination of both (about 4 sausages)
- 1 large onion, chopped (1 cup)
- 1 clove garlic, minced
- 1 can (16 ounces) tomatoes
- 1 can (6 ounces) tomato paste
- 1 cup water
- ¾ teaspoon leaf basil, crumbled
- ¾ teaspoon leaf oregano, crumbled
- 1 teaspoon salt
- ¼ teaspoon pepper

1. Remove casings from sausages; cook meat slowly in a medium-size saucepan, breaking up with a spoon as it cooks until no pink remains. Remove with slotted spoon to paper toweling to drain. Remove all but 1 tablespoon drippings from pan.
2. Sauté onion and garlic in drippings until tender, about 5 minutes. Return sausage to saucepan; add tomatoes, tomato paste, water, basil, oregano, salt and pepper. Bring to boiling; lower heat; simmer sauce, stirring occasionally, 30 minutes or until thickened.

QUICK RED CLAM SAUCE

Makes about 3 cups.

- 1 large onion, chopped (1 cup)
- 4 cloves garlic, minced
- ¼ cup olive or vegetable oil
- 2 cans (6½ to 8 ounces each) minced clams
- 6 medium-size tomatoes, peeled and coarsely chopped
- 1 teaspoon salt
- ½ teaspoon pepper
- ½ teaspoon leaf basil, crumbled
- ½ teaspoon leaf oregano, crumbled
- 2 tablespoons chopped fresh parsley

Sauté onion and garlic in olive oil in a medium-size saucepan until soft. Drain liquid from clams into saucepan, reserving clams. Add tomatoes, salt, pepper, basil and oregano; bring to boiling; lower heat. Simmer, uncovered, 15 minutes, stirring occasionally, until sauce is thickened the way you like it. Mix in clams and parsley and heat 5 minutes longer.

HOMEMADE MEAT SAUCE

Makes 12 cups.

- 1 large onion, chopped (1 cup)
- 2 cloves garlic, minced
- ¼ cup vegetable oil
- 1 pound ground round or chuck
- 2 Italian sausages, chopped
- 2 cans (35 ounces each) plum tomatoes
- 2 cans (6 ounces each) tomato paste
- 2 tablespoons sugar
- 1 tablespoon leaf oregano, crumbled
- 1 tablespoon leaf basil, crumbled
- 1 tablespoon salt
- ½ teaspoon pepper
- ¼ cup grated Parmesan cheese

1. Sauté onion and garlic in oil until soft in a large skillet; brown beef and sausage in same skillet. Pour off all but 2 tablespoons drippings.
2. Stir in tomatoes, tomato paste, sugar, oregano, basil, salt and pepper. Simmer, uncovered, stirring frequently, 45 minutes or until sauce thickens. Stir in Parmesan cheese.

Sauce

LEMON-PARSLEY CLAM SAUCE

The tangy flavor of lemon gives character to this quick clam sauce for linguine.

Makes 1½ cups.

- 2 cans (6½ to 8 ounces each) minced clams
- 1 small onion, chopped (¼ cup)
- 3 cloves garlic, minced
- ⅓ cup olive or vegetable oil
- 2 tablespoons butter or margarine
- 1 teaspoon leaf oregano, crumbled
- ½ teaspoon salt
- ⅛ teaspoon pepper
- 2 tablespoons chopped fresh parsley
- 1 teaspoon grated lemon rind
- 1 to 2 tablespoons lemon juice

1. Drain clam juice from clams; reserve.
2. Sauté onion and garlic in oil and butter in a saucepan until tender, but not brown, about 5 minutes.
3. Add reserved clam juice, oregano, salt and pepper; bring to boiling over high heat. Cook until reduced to 1 cup, about 5 minutes.
4. Lower heat under clam juice mixture; add reserved clams, parsley, lemon rind and lemon juice; heat thoroughly.

CHINESE SWEET-SOUR SAUCE

Makes 1¼ cups.

- ¼ cup firmly packed brown sugar
- 2 tablespoons cornstarch
- ½ teaspoon seasoned salt
- ¾ cup pineapple juice
- ¼ cup water
- 2 tablespoons cider vinegar
- 2 tablespoons honey
- 2 teaspoons soy sauce

1. Mix brown sugar, cornstarch and seasoned salt in a small saucepan; blend in pineapple juice, water, cider vinegar, honey and soy sauce. Cook and stir until the sauce thickens and bubbles 1 minute.
2. Pour over crisp-cooked vegetables in a large skillet; toss to mix well; cover. (See Note.)
3. Simmer 5 to 8 minutes or just until the vegetables are tender.

Note: To prepare and crisp-cook the vegetables, cut pared carrots into thin pennies, green pepper into very thin rings and cabbage into thin shreds. (You should have about 6 cups.) Heat 2 tablespoons of vegetable oil in a large skillet. Add vegetables; toss to coat with oil. Cook and stir 2 to 3 minutes or until shiny-moist.

ORANGE-SPICE BARBECUE SAUCE

It gives a golden-glaze goodness to grilled ducklings. Delicious with pork chops and chicken, too.

Makes 1½ cups.

- ¼ cup sugar
- 2 tablespoons cornstarch
- ½ teaspoon ground allspice
- ½ teaspoon ground cloves
- 1 cup orange juice
- 2 tablespoons cider vinegar
- ¼ cup (½ stick) butter or margarine

Combine sugar, cornstarch, allspice and cloves in a small saucepan; stir in orange juice and vinegar. Cook, stirring constantly, until sauce thickens and bubbles for 1 minute. Stir in butter until blended.

DUCK SAUCE

This is sweet and sharp—ideal for roast duckling.

Makes 1 cup.

- 1 cup plum jam
- 1 tablespoon cider vinegar
- 1 teaspoon grated onion
- ½ teaspoon ground allspice
- ¼ teaspoon ground ginger
- Dash cayenne

1. Combine the jam, vinegar, onion, allspice, ginger and cayenne in small saucepan; heat, stirring constantly, just to boiling.
2. Cool, then chill. This sauce keeps well in the refrigerator.

HOT FUDGE SAUCE

The real fudgy kind that stiffens when it's poured on cold ice cream.

Makes about 2 cups.

- 4 squares unsweetened chocolate
- 2 tablespoons butter or margarine
- ¾ cup boiling water
- 2 cups sugar
- 3 tablespoons corn syrup
- 2 teaspoons vanilla

1. Coarsely chop chocolate; heat with butter and boiling water in a large heavy saucepan over low heat, stirring constantly, until chocolate is melted. Add sugar and corn syrup.
2. Bring mixture slowly to boiling; lower heat; simmer gently for 7 to 8 minutes. Watch carefully, but do not stir. Test on ice cream or an ice cube, until it firms up as you like it. Add vanilla. Serve while warm. Refrigerate any leftover sauce in canning jar; cover.
3. To reheat: Remove cover from jar. Place jar in saucepan of water; cover. Heat, stirring occasionally, until sauce is softened enough to pour. This sauce is great on ice cream, pound cake, ice cream-filled meringue shells and banana splits.

APRICOT BRANDY SAUCE

Makes about 2 cups.

- 1½ cups apricot preserves
- ⅓ cup water
- 2 tablespoons sugar
- 2 tablespoons brandy

Combine apricot preserves, water and sugar in a medium-size saucepan. Bring to boiling; boil 15 minutes or until slightly thickened. Puree in a blender or food processor; add brandy. Serve warm.

HOT LEMON SAUCE

Makes 1⅓ cups.

- ½ cup sugar
- 1 tablespoon cornstarch
- 1 cup water
- 1 tablespoon butter or margarine
- 2 tablespoons lemon juice
- ½ teaspoon grated lemon rind

Combine sugar and cornstarch in medium-size saucepan. Stir in water. Cook over moderate heat 5 minutes, stirring constantly with wire whisk, until smooth and bubbly. Add butter, lemon juice and rind. Stir until butter is melted. This can be made ahead of time and then reheated just before serving.

Pictured opposite: Hot Fudge Sauce, page 606; Raspberry Sauce, page 608; Creamy Custard Sauce, page 608

Sauce

CREAMY CUSTARD SAUCE

Makes 1½ cups.

- 3 egg yolks
- 3 tablespoons sugar
- ¾ cup milk, scalded
- 1 teaspoon vanilla
- ½ cup heavy cream, whipped

1. Beat egg yolks and sugar until light and fluffy in small bowl with electric mixer. Gradually beat in scalded milk. Pour mixture back into saucepan; cook, stirring constantly, over moderate heat until custard thickens slightly. Remove from heat; pour into small bowl; stir in vanilla; cover; chill.
2. Just before serving, fold in whipped cream.

RASPBERRY SAUCE

Makes 1¼ cups.

- 1 package (10 ounces) frozen red raspberries, thawed
- ¼ cup sugar
- 2 tablespoons kirsch or light rum

Put raspberries into the container of an electric blender; add sugar; cover; blend on high speed until smooth. Strain through a sieve over bowl to remove seeds. Cover with plastic wrap; chill. Stir in kirsch just before serving.

———— •●• ————

SAUERBRATEN A German favorite, sauerbraten means "sour roast." Beef is marinated in a spicy vinegar mixture then pot-roasted slowly until tender. The sauce is thickened with gingersnap crumbs. Traditionally, sauerbraten is served with either potato dumplings or potato pancakes and red cabbage.

OLD GERMAN SAUERBRATEN

Makes 10 to 12 servings.

- 1 boneless round, rump, sirloin tip or chuck roast (5 to 6 pounds), rolled and tied
- 2 cups wine vinegar or cider vinegar
- 2 cups water
- ¼ cup firmly packed brown sugar
- 1 tablespoon salt
- ½ teaspoon pepper
- ½ teaspoon ground cloves
- 1 bay leaf
- 3 medium-size onions, chopped (1½ cups)
- 2 large carrots, pared and diced (1½ cups)
- 1½ cups diced celery
- 2 tablespoons bacon drippings or vegetable shortening (optional)
- 8 gingersnaps, crumbled
  Potato Dumplings (recipe follows)
  Parsley sprigs

1. Place meat in a large bowl; add vinegar, water, brown sugar, salt, pepper, cloves, bay leaf, onions, carrots and celery. Cover; store in refrigerator 2 to 3 days, turning meat several times to marinate on all sides.
2. When ready to cook, remove meat from marinade and pat dry; brown in its own fat or in bacon drippings in large, heavy kettle or Dutch oven; add vegetables and marinade. Bring to boiling; cover.
3. Simmer 3 hours or until meat is very tender. Remove to a heated serving platter and keep hot.
4. Strain broth into a 4-cup measure; let stand about 1 minute or until fat rises to top. Skim off fat, returning ¼ cup to kettle.
5. Add water to broth, if needed, to make 2 cups; stir back into kettle; sprinkle crumbled gingersnaps over. Cook and stir until gravy thickens.
6. Arrange Potato Dumplings on platter with meat. Spoon gravy over dumplings. Serve with cooked red cabbage and apple slices, if you wish. Garnish platter with parsley.

POTATO DUMPLINGS

Makes 6 servings (12 dumplings).

- 1 slice white bread
- 1 tablespoon butter or margarine
- 3 medium-size potatoes (1½ pounds)
- 2 eggs, slightly beaten
- ⅓ cup *sifted* all-purpose flour
- ⅓ cup dry cream of wheat cereal
- 1½ teaspoons salt
- ¼ teaspoon pepper
- ¼ teaspoon ground nutmeg

1. Cut bread slice into ½-inch cubes. Melt butter or margarine in small skillet; add bread and sauté until golden brown.
2. Peel potatoes; cook in boiling water in a large saucepan until tender, about 20 minutes. Drain; return to saucepan; toss over low heat for several minutes to dry. Remove from heat.
3. Mash potatoes (there should be about 3 cups); beat in eggs, flour, cream of wheat, salt, pepper and nutmeg until smooth.
4. Heat 3 to 4 quarts water to boiling in a large kettle. Divide potato mixture into 12 equal parts; shape each around 3 or 4 of the bread cubes into a round ball, dusting hands with flour to keep dumplings from sticking.
5. Drop dumplings into boiling water; stir gently once or twice to prevent them from sticking to each other or the bottom of the kettle. Cook, uncovered, until dumplings float to surface of water, about 10 to 15 minutes; remove with slotted spoon to heated platter and spoon a little gravy over each.

———— •●• ————

SAUERKRAUT Thinly shredded cabbage, salted and fermented in its own juice drawn out by salt. Sauerkraut is called *choucroute* by the French of Alsace in northeastern France and served garnished with a variety of smoked meats. Sauerkraut is equally popular with Germans and the Austrians who gave it its name.

Sauerkraut, however, is not native to Europe. Its origin was in China some 2,000 years ago during the construction of the Great Wall. The workers ate pickled cabbage with rice. When the Tartars invaded China they tasted the pickled cabbage and introduced it to eastern Europe —where it has become a popular vegetable. From there, sauerkraut was made in many countries. German immigrants were the first to make sauerkraut in America.

Sauerkraut is a tasty accompaniment to frankfurters, pork, ham, spareribs and other sausages. It is marketed in cans or refrigerated packages. Sauerkraut can be rinsed with cold water and drained to remove some of the briny taste.

Pictured opposite: Old German Sauerbraten, page 608

Sauerkraut

CHOUCROUTE À L'ALSACIENNE

A classic dinner of sauerkraut, pork-shoulder roll and sausages.

Bake at 350° for 2 hours, 20 minutes.
Makes 8 servings.

- 2 cans (27 ounces each) sauerkraut
- 1 smoked pork shoulder roll (about 2 pounds)
- 2 carrots, finely chopped (1 cup)
- 1 large onion, chopped (1 cup)
- 1 can (12 ounces) light beer
- 1 can condensed beef broth
- 1 pound knockwursts or frankfurters
- 6 parsley sprigs
- 4 whole peppercorns
- 1 bay leaf
- 2 tart cooking apples, quartered, cored and sliced
  Boiled red potatoes

1. Soak sauerkraut for 5 minutes in a large pan of cold water; change the water twice; drain well.
2. Remove casing from pork shoulder. Brown in a 12-cup flameproof, baking dish. Remove from dish. Sauté carrot and onion until soft in pan drippings. Stir in drained sauerkraut; toss to blend well.
3. Return browned pork shoulder to dish. Pour beer and beef broth over. Score sausages; place over sauerkraut.
4. Tie parsley, peppercorns and bay leaf in a piece of cheesecloth. Push under liquid in dish; cover.
5. Bake in a moderate oven (350°) for 2 hours; toss in apple slices. Bake 20 minutes longer or until pork is tender and liquid absorbed. Discard herb bag.
6. Remove pork shoulder and cut into thick slices. Spoon sauerkraut, apples and sausages into heated serving dish. Arrange pork slices and a few boiled potatoes on top. Pass remaining potatoes, along with sharp mustard and chunks of pumpernickel bread.

SAUERKRAUT RELISH

Makes about 1 quart.

- 1 can (27 ounces) sauerkraut, drained (about 3½ cups)
- ¼ cup sugar
- ¼ cup honey
- 2 tablespoons vegetable oil
- 1 teaspoon caraway seeds
- ¼ teaspoon salt
  Dash pepper
- ⅓ cup finely chopped onion
- 3 tablespoons chopped canned pimiento

Combine sauerkraut, sugar, honey, oil, caraway seeds, salt, pepper and onion in a large saucepan. Simmer, covered, 20 minutes; stir in pimiento. Turn into a jar. Cover. Cool; chill at least 4 hours. Keep refrigerated. Will keep for about a week.

EASY "CHOUCROUTE GARNI"

Not the classic recipe, but a hearty and satisfying substitute.

Makes 6 to 8 servings.

- 1 package (¾ ounce) brown gravy mix
- ⅓ cup firmly packed dark brown sugar
- 1 teaspoon caraway seeds
- ½ cup beer
- 1 medium-size onion, thinly sliced
- 2 bratwursts
- 2 knockwursts
- 1 package (1 pound) chicken frankfurters, halved
- 2 packages (16 ounces each) fresh sauerkraut
- 1 can (20 ounces) sliced apples, drained

Combine gravy mix, brown sugar, caraway seeds and beer in large skillet. Add onion, bratwursts, knockwursts and franks. Simmer, stirring and turning meats for about 20 minutes. Add sauerkraut; mix well. Cook over medium heat 10 minutes. Add sliced apples. Cook until thoroughly heated.

———— ●●● ————

SAUSAGE Ground meat usually enclosed in a casing. Sausages have been made since antiquity and many countries are noted for their own special sausages. Some are named for the city of origin, such as the frankfurter for Frankfurt, Germany and the bologna for Bologna, Italy.

Sausages may be fresh or smoked, dry or semi-dry, uncooked or fully cooked. With such an enormous variety of sausages, they can be served for any meal.

HOT SAUSAGE AND MOZZARELLA ROLL

Bake at 375° for 30 minutes.
Makes 8 servings.

- 2 loaves (1 pound each) frozen plain bread dough
- 1½ pounds hot Italian sausages, casings removed
- 1 large onion, chopped (1 cup)
- 1 package (8 ounces) mozzarella cheese, shredded
- ¼ cup freshly grated Parmesan cheese
- ¼ cup chopped fresh parsley
- 1 egg yolk beaten with 2 tablespoons water
- 2 tablespoons sesame seeds *(optional)*

1. Thaw dough in refrigerator overnight or at room temperature for about 1 hour, just until soft enough to yield to pressure of a fingerprint.
2. Meanwhile, prepare filling: Place sausages and onion in a large skillet; cook 10 minutes, stirring often, breaking up meat with the side of a spoon. Transfer sausage and onion to a plate with a slotted spoon; refrigerate.
3. Pat out 1 piece of dough to flatten on a lightly floured surface. Roll dough into a 14×9-inch rectangle; sprinkle with half the cooled sausage, cheeses and parsley. Roll up dough starting with 1 long side, enclosing filling like a jelly roll. Preheat oven to 375°.
4. Transfer roll, seam-side down, to a lightly greased cookie sheet and tuck ends under. Brush with egg mixture. Repeat with remaining dough and filling; place second roll several inches from first on same cookie sheet. Brush with egg mixture; sprinkle with sesame seeds, if you wish.
5. Bake in a preheated moderate oven (375°) for 30 minutes or until crust is golden brown.
6. Remove loaves to a serving platter and cut into 1½-inch slices to serve.

SAUSAGES IN ONION AND APPLE SAUCE

Makes 6 servings.

- **6 tablespoons butter**
- **4 large onions, thinly sliced**
- **1 teaspoon salt**
- **¼ teaspoon pepper**
  Large pinch sugar
- **12 fresh pork sausages**
- **½ cup dry white wine**
- **3 Golden Delicious apples, pared, quartered and cored**
  Sugar
  Salt
  Ground nutmeg

1. Heat 2 tablespoons of the butter in a large skillet. Add onions, salt, pepper and sugar. Cook over low heat for 40 minutes, stirring occasionally, until onions are soft and nicely browned. Remove onions with a slotted spoon.
2. Add 2 more tablespoons of butter to skillet. Cook sausages over medium heat, turning occasionally, 10 minutes or until nicely browned and cooked through. Remove from skillet.
3. Pour off all fat from skillet. Add wine, stirring and scraping any brown bits in the skillet. Cook until wine is reduced to 2 tablespoons. Return onions and sausages to skillet; cover; simmer 10 minutes.
4. While sausages are simmering, heat remaining butter in a small skillet. Add the apples, sprinkle with sugar, a pinch of salt and nutmeg. Cook 5 to 6 minutes, shaking the pan occasionally, until apples are soft and lightly browned. Add apples to sausage mixture in skillet.

ITALIAN SAUSAGE STRATA

Bake at 325° for 1 hour.
Makes 4 servings.

- **½ pound Italian sausages (sweet, hot or combination)**
- **½ cup chopped green pepper**
- **1 medium-size onion, chopped (½ cup)**
- **1 can (16 ounces) tomatoes, drained**
- **½ loaf Italian bread**
- **3 eggs**
- **2½ cups milk**
- **1 teaspoon salt**
- **1 tablespoon grated Parmesan cheese**

1. Remove casing from sausages. Brown sausages in a large skillet about 10 minutes, breaking it up with a wooden spoon as it browns. Stir in green pepper and onion. Cook another 5 minutes; add tomatoes, breaking up pieces. Cook 15 minutes to remove most of the liquid.
2. Slice bread; place half the slices in bottom of buttered 8 × 8 × 2-inch baking pan; spread with meat mixture. Top with remaining bread.
3. Beat eggs in medium-size bowl. Stir in milk and salt. Pour over bread. Sprinkle with cheese. Cover and refrigerate at least 1 hour or overnight.
4. Bake in a moderate oven (325°) for 1 hour or until puffed and golden. Remove to wire rack. Let stand 10 minutes before serving.

SAUSAGE-SPAGHETTI BAKE

Chunks of sweet Italian sausage are the "meatballs" in this easy-serve specialty.

Bake at 375° for 30 minutes.
Makes 6 servings.

- **1 pound sweet Italian sausages, sliced in 1-inch pieces**
- **1 clove garlic, minced**
- **1 can (35 ounces) plum tomatoes**
- **1 can (8 ounces) tomato sauce**
- **½ cup water**
- **1 teaspoon sugar**
- **½ teaspoon Italian herb seasoning mix, crumbled**
- **1 package (1 pound) thin spaghetti**
- **½ cup grated Parmesan cheese**

1. Brown sausages slowly in large skillet; push to one side. Add the garlic and sauté 2 minutes; pour off all fat.
2. Stir in tomatoes, tomato sauce, water, sugar and herb seasoning. Bring to boiling; simmer, covered, for 30 minutes to blend flavors.
3. While sauce simmers, cook spaghetti following label directions; drain well.
4. Spoon about half of spaghetti into a 13 × 9 × 2-inch baking dish; top with half of the meat sauce. Repeat with remaining spaghetti and sauce to make 2 layers of each; sprinkle with cheese.
5. Bake in a moderate oven (375°) for 30 minutes or until bubbly-hot. Let stand for 5 minutes, then cut into 6 equal-size servings. Lift out with wide spatula.

PIONEER SAUSAGE BURGER STEW

Makes 6 servings.

- **¼ pound (½ cup) liver sausage**
- **1 pound ground chuck or round**
- **½ cup packaged bread crumbs**
- **1 small onion, finely chopped (¼ cup)**
- **1 egg, beaten**
- **3 tablespoons vegetable oil**
- **2 tablespoons flour**
- **½ teaspoon salt**
- **2 envelopes or teaspoons instant beef broth**
- **2 cups hot water**
- **4 cups thinly sliced zucchini**
- **3 cups seasoned hot mashed potatoes**
- **1 medium-size tomato, cut in thin wedges**
  Paprika

1. Mash liver sausage with fork in a large bowl. Add beef, crumbs, onion and egg; mix well. Divide mixture and shape into 12 balls, using about ¼ cup for each. Brown meatballs in oil in a large skillet; remove and keep warm.
2. Pour off all but 2 tablespoons of drippings from skillet. Stir in flour and salt; cook 1 minute. Combine instant broth and water in a 2-cup measure; pour into skillet. Cook, stirring constantly, until sauce is slightly thickened. Return meatballs to skillet. Cover; cook slowly for 10 minutes. Add zucchini; cook 10 minutes longer, stirring gently once or twice.
3. Spoon or pipe mashed potatoes around edge of skillet and arrange tomato wedges on top. Sprinkle potatoes with paprika. If skillet isn't flameproof, wrap handle with foil. Place skillet under broiler to heat and brown potatoes lightly, about 5 minutes.

Sausage

JUMBO STACK BRAUNSCHWEIGER SANDWICH

Makes 6 sandwiches.

- 6 large slices Italian or rye bread, toasted, if desired
  Dill Mustard Sauce *(recipe follows)*
  Lettuce leaves
- 12 slices liver sausage or Braunschweiger (about 1 pound)
- 12 thin tomato slices
- 12 thin cucumber slices
- 12 thin onion slices

Spread bread or toast with Dill Mustard Sauce. Top one bread slice with lettuce and overlapping slices of liver sausage, tomato, cucumber and onion, using 2 slices of each for each sandwich. Serve open-face.

DILL MUSTARD SAUCE

Makes 1 cup.

- ⅓ cup dairy sour cream
- ⅓ cup mayonnaise or salad dressing
- 3 tablespoons prepared mustard
- 3 tablespoons chopped dill pickle

Combine ingredients in small bowl.

SAUSAGE PÂTÈ EN CROÛTE

Makes about 12 servings.

- 1 large loaf rye, white or Italian bread
  OR: 2 loaves (7 ounces each) French bread
- 1 package (8 ounces) cream cheese
- 1 pound liver sausage
- 2 tablespoons brandy
- ¼ cup pistachio nuts *(optional)*
- ¼ pound unsliced ham, tongue or bologna, cut into ½-inch cubes

1. Slice about ½ inch off each end of loaf of bread. Hollow out inside with serrated knife and long-handled fork, leaving ½-inch crust all around. (Use crumbs for another recipe.)
2. Soften cream cheese in a large bowl. Cut sausage in chunks and add to cheese; add brandy. Beat with electric mixer until smooth; stir in pistachios. Fold diced meat into sausage mixture.
3. Pack pâtè mixture into hollowed

bread. Press both end slices back onto loaf. Wrap loaf in foil and chill several hours. Cut loaf in slices about ½-inch thick and garnish with parsley and tomatoes or, for a festive touch, fresh grapes.

SAUSAGE-EGG PITA

Makes 4 servings.

- 1 package (8 ounces) brown-and-serve sausage links, thinly sliced
- 4 eggs
- ½ cup dairy sour cream
- 1 tablespoon chopped chives
- ⅛ teaspoon pepper
- 2 tablespoons butter or margarine
- 2 large pita breads, halved crosswise

1. Cook sausage slices in large skillet over medium heat until lightly browned, stirring frequently. Remove from heat; drain sausage slices on paper toweling.
2. Combine eggs, sour cream, chives and pepper in large bowl. Stir in sausages.
3. Melt butter in same skillet. Add sausage-egg mixture and cook just until firm, yet moist, stirring gently with pancake turner.
4. Spoon into pita bread pockets. Serve with sliced cherry tomatoes, if you wish.

SAUSAGE-STUFFED ZUCCHINI

Bake at 350° for 30 minutes.
Makes 4 servings.

- 8 medium-size zucchini (about 3½ pounds)
- 1 pound sweet Italian sausages
- 1 large onion, finely chopped (1 cup)
- ¼ cup chopped fresh parsley
- 1 teaspoon leaf basil, crumbled
- ½ teaspoon salt
- ¼ teaspoon pepper
- ½ cup grated Parmesan cheese
- ½ cup packaged bread crumbs
- 2 eggs, slightly beaten

1. Halve zucchini lengthwise. Cook in boiling water in a kettle or Dutch oven just until barely tender, about 10 minutes. Drain; scoop out seeds with tip of teaspoon, leaving shell about ¼- to

½-inch thick. Chop the scooped-out portion very finely.
2. Remove casings from sausages; cook sausages slowly in a large skillet, breaking it up with a spoon as it cooks, until no trace of pink remains. Stir in onion, parsley, basil, salt and pepper. Cook, stirring occasionally, until onion is tender, about 5 minutes.
3. Remove from heat; stir in chopped zucchini, Parmesan, bread crumbs and eggs, mixing well. Fill shells with mixture, dividing equally and mounding slightly. Arrange shells close together in a 13 × 9 × 2-inch baking pan.
4. Bake in a moderate oven (350°) for 30 minutes or just until filling is hot.

BEEF SAUSAGE OVER EGGS

Makes 4 servings.

- 1 pound ground chuck
- 1 small onion, grated
- ¼ cup cold water
- 1½ teaspoons salt
- 1½ teaspoons leaf marjoram, crumbled
- ½ teaspoon ground allspice
- ¼ teaspoon ground nutmeg
- ⅛ teaspoon cayenne
- 8 eggs
- ⅓ cup milk
- ⅛ teaspoon pepper
- 2 tablespoons butter or margarine

1. Combine beef, onion, water, 1 teaspoon of the salt, marjoram, allspice, nutmeg and cayenne in a medium-size bowl until well mixed. Shape into roll about 2½ inches in diameter and 7 inches long. Wrap in wax paper; chill several hours or overnight until firm enough for slicing.
2. Cut sausage roll into ½-inch slices with a sharp knife. Cook slices in skillet until well browned, turning often.
3. While sausage cooks, beat eggs, milk, remaining ½ teaspoon salt and pepper in medium-size bowl. Melt butter in large skillet. Add beaten eggs; cook until eggs are thickened but still moist. Transfer to platter; arrange sausages on top.

●●●

Scallop

SAUTERNE An American-made sauterne is either a sweet or dry white wine. French sauternes (spelled with the final "s"), is a sweet white wine from the Sauternes district of Bordeaux. Sauterne is best served cold, but not iced, at the end of a meal with a dessert or with fruit.

SAVARIN The French name for the Italian baba au rhum, a yeast cake baked in a mold, soaked in sugar syrup flavored with a spirit. Savarin is usually ring-shaped and may be flavored with kirsch instead of rum.

SAVORY There are two closely related savory plants that are grown for their aromatic leaves. Summer savory is an annual with narrow, ½- to 1½-inch-long leaves. Winter savory is a perennial with stiff, narrow to round leaves that are ½- to 1-inch long. They are members of the mint family of herbs. See also **HERBS**

Savory leaves are sometimes available fresh but more commonly they are dried, either crushed or ground. They have a pleasant peppery taste that complements bean dishes, poultry, pork, soups and stews. Summer savory is more delicate than the winter variety and is used more frequently. Ground savory is an ingredient in poultry seasoning.

SCALLION See **ONION**.

SCALLOP It's unfortunate that only the fishermen see the scallop's beautiful fan-shaped, fluted shell. Unlike other bivalved mollusks such as clams, oysters and mussels, scallops are more highly perishable. A scallop cannot keep its shell tightly closed when removed from the water. It loses moisture and as a result will die. So, only the muscle which opens and closes the shell is sold for food. The rest of the scallop's body is discarded. In Europe, scallops are sold in their shells and the entire body is eaten.

There are two varieties: The tiny bay scallops, usually ½ inch in diameter; and the larger, less expensive sea scallops that can measure up to 2 inches across. Bay scallops, which have a more delicate flavor and a more tender texture, are not as readily available as sea scallops. The larger sea scallops, which are best for broiling, have a somewhat stronger flavor and firmer texture. There are color differences among scallops harvested from different waters. Color of the flesh can range from a white to cream to yellow-orange.

Scallops are low in calories (81 calories for 3½-ounces raw) but rich in iodine and phosphorous as well as in protein. They cook quickly and there is no waste in preparation.

Buying and Storing: Fresh sea scallops are available in fish markets along the coasts of the United States, or major inland cities if they are flown in. They are also sold frozen, either plain or breaded and fried. In the northeastern part of this country, bay scallops are marketed fresh from mid-September until mid-April.

The freshness of scallops can be judged by smell and sight. Scallops should have a sweet aroma. Their surface should be moist and shiny and they should not be swimming in liquid. Fresh scallops should be stored in the coldest part of the refrigerator and used within 2 days.

SWEET AND SOUR SCALLOP KEBOBS

Bake at 400° for 22 minutes.
Makes 6 servings.

- 1 package (6¼ ounces) fried rice mix with vermicelli and almonds
  OR: 1 package (7 ounces) instant fried rice mix
- 1 package (10 ounces) frozen Brussels sprouts, partially thawed and each halved
- 1 can (16 ounces) whole carrots, drained
- 1 tablespoon vegetable oil
- 2 packages (8 ounces each) frozen batter-fried scallops, partially thawed
- ¾ cup apricot or peach preserves
- 3 tablespoons sweet and spicy bottled French dressing
- 2 tablespoons prepared mustard
- ½ teaspoon ground ginger

1. Cook rice mix following label directions; keep warm. Preheat oven to 400°.
2. Gently toss Brussels sprouts and carrots with oil in large bowl. Thread scallops, sprouts and carrots alternately on six 15-inch metal skewers. Place on foil-lined jelly-roll pan, allowing the skewers to rest on the edge of pan so that the ingredients do not touch bottom of pan.
3. Bake in a preheated hot oven (400°) for 20 minutes.
4. Combine preserves, French dressing, mustard and ginger in a small saucepan; bring to boiling. Brush some of the sauce over kebobs; bake 2 minutes more or until glazed.
5. Spoon rice on warm platter; arrange kebobs on top. Pass remaining sauce.

SEVICHE

Makes about 4½ cups or about 8 appetizer servings.

- 1 cup fresh lime juice
- 3 medium-size tomatoes, seeded and chopped (about 3 cups)
- 1 medium-size onion, chopped (½ cup)
- ½ green pepper, halved, seeded and chopped (½ cup)
- 2 canned mild or hot green chilies, chopped
- 3 cloves garlic, finely chopped
- 1½ teaspoons salt
- ¼ teaspoon freshly ground pepper
- 1 pound fresh bay or sea scallops*, washed
- 8 lettuce cups

1. Combine lime juice, tomatoes, onion, green pepper, chilies, garlic, salt and pepper in medium-size bowl; mix well.
2. Gently stir in scallops. (If using sea scallops, cut into quarters.)
3. Chill 3 hours or overnight. Serve in lettuce cups.

*If fresh scallops are not available in your area, use fresh flounder or halibut fillets, and cut into bite-size pieces.

SCALLOP CHOWDER

Makes about 6 servings.

  1 **package (12 ounces) frozen scallops**
  3 **cups boiling water**
  1 **teaspoon salt**
  2 **cups cubed potatoes (about 2 medium)**
  1 **cup cubed carrots (3 medium)**
  1 **cup sliced celery**
  1 **medium-size onion, chopped (½ cup)**
  1 **cup milk**
  1 **cup chicken broth**
  ⅛ **teaspoon white pepper**
  2 **tablespoons butter or margarine**
    Lemon slices

1. Cook frozen scallops in boiling, salted water for 3 minutes or until tender; remove from water with slotted spoon; reserve.
2. Add potatoes, carrots, celery and onion to same water; simmer until tender, about 10 minutes. Stir in milk, chicken broth, pepper and butter. Puree in blender with ½ cup of the scallops. Return to pan with remaining whole scallops and reheat. Garnish with lemon slices.

COQUILLES ST. JACQUES MORNAY

Makes 4 servings as main dish, 6 to 8 as an appetizer.

  1 **cup dry white wine**
  ½ **teaspoon salt**
  1 **pound fresh or thawed, frozen sea scallops, washed**
  2 **tablespoons chopped onion**
  ¼ **pound small mushrooms, sliced**
  ¼ **cup butter or margarine**
  ¼ **cup all-purpose flour**
  ½ **cup heavy cream**
  2 **teaspoons lemon juice**
  ⅓ **cup shredded Swiss cheese**
  1 **tablespoon chopped fresh parsley**
  ½ **cup fresh bread crumbs (1 slice)**
  1 **tablespoon melted butter or margarine**
    Parsley
    Lemon wedges

1. Bring wine to boiling in small saucepan. Lower heat; add the salt and scallops; cover. Simmer until just tender, 5 to 6 minutes. Drain, reserving liquid (1 cup).
2. Sauté onion and mushrooms until soft in butter in medium-size saucepan, then remove from heat; stir in the flour until smooth; gradually stir in reserved liquid. Cook, stirring constantly, until sauce thickens and bubbles. Stir in cream and lemon juice. Bring to boiling; remove from heat. If sauce is too thick, add more cream or wine. Taste and add more salt or lemon juice, if necessary.
3. Add scallops, cheese and parsley to sauce; spoon into 4 buttered scallop shells or 1-cup casseroles, dividing evenly.
4. Toss bread crumbs with melted butter; sprinkle crumbs around edge of the shells. Place shells on rack over broiler pan. Broil 4 to 6 inches from heat for 4 minutes or until crumbs are brown and sauce bubbles. Garnish with parsley and lemon wedges.

SHRIMP AND SCALLOPS IN WINE SAUCE

Delicately pink and temptingly tender, this shellfish combination tastes as good as it looks.

Makes 8 servings.

  1½ **cups dry white wine**
  ½ **cup clam juice or water**
  1 **bay leaf**
  1 **pound fresh or thawed, frozen shelled and deveined shrimp, washed**
  1 **pound fresh or thawed, frozen scallops, washed (large sea scallops should be quartered)**
  1 **small onion, finely chopped (¼ cup)**
  3 **tablespoons butter or margarine**
  ¼ **cup all-purpose flour**
  ½ **teaspoon salt**
  2 **tablespoons tomato paste***
  1 **cup light cream or half-and-half**
  1 **package (10 ounces) frozen puff pastry shells, baked following label directions**

1. Combine wine, clam juice and bay leaf in large saucepan; bring to boiling; add shrimp and scallops. After mixture comes to the boil again, lower heat; simmer 3 minutes or just until shrimp and scallops are firm-tender. Drain, reserving cooking liquid.
2. Sauté onion in butter in a large saucepan just until tender but not browned; stir in flour and salt until mixture is smooth. Gradually stir in reserved cooking liquid and tomato paste. Cook, stirring constantly, until mixture thickens and bubbles. Lower heat; simmer 5 minutes.
3. Add cream, shrimp and scallops; place over low heat just until heated through. Serve in pastry shells. Garnish with lemon and watercress, if you wish.

*To keep opened tomato paste for a future use, measure paste by tablespoonfuls onto a small sheet of foil; freeze. When solid, store pieces in plastic bag and keep frozen.

HERB-BAKED SCALLOPS

Bake at 350° for 25 minutes.
Makes 6 servings.

  2 **pounds fresh or thawed, frozen sea scallops**
  ½ **cup (1 stick) butter or margarine**
  3 **tablespoons chopped fresh parsley**
  1½ **teaspoons leaf basil, crumbled**
  1 **teaspoon salt**
  ¼ **teaspoon pepper**

1. Preheat oven to 350°. Wash the scallops in cold water and drain thoroughly between sheets of paper toweling.
2. Place the scallops in a single layer in a large, shallow, baking dish; dot with the butter; sprinkle with parsley, basil, salt and pepper.
3. Bake in a preheated moderate oven (350°) for 5 minutes. Stir scallops to coat well with butter mixture. Bake 20 minutes longer or until tender. Serve the buttery sauce from dish over mashed or baked potatoes, if you wish.

●●●

SCALOPPINE The Italian term for thin slices of meat, usually veal, that are flattened and fried. Nowadays, chicken, turkey or pork are used in place of veal. The English word for scaloppine is "escallop."

VEAL SCALOPPINE MARSALA

Quickly brown the thinly sliced meat, then top with a delicate wine sauce and serve over rice.

Makes 8 servings.

- ½ **cup all-purpose flour**
- 2 **pounds veal for scaloppine**
- ¼ **cup (½ stick) butter or margarine**
- ⅔ **cup dry Marsala**
- ½ **teaspoon salt**
- ⅛ **teaspoon pepper**
- 1 **envelope or teaspoon instant beef broth**

1. Place flour on wax paper. Dip veal slices into flour to coat lightly.
2. Sauté veal, a few pieces at a time, in part of the butter in a large skillet just until lightly browned. Remove from pan to a plate as they brown; keep warm. Add butter as needed.
3. Stir Marsala into skillet, scraping browned bits from bottom of pan. Stir in salt, pepper and instant beef broth. Simmer 2 minutes.
4. Return veal to skillet; cover. Simmer 5 minutes. Serve with hot cooked rice, if you wish.

SCALOPPINE WITH PEPPERS

The charm of this simple dish is the crisp bite of peppers.

Makes 4 servings.

- 2 **whole chicken breasts (about 14 ounces each), boned, skinned and halved**
  - OR: 4 **rib pork chops (each ½-inch thick), boned**
- ½ **teaspoon salt**
- ¼ **teaspoon pepper**
  Flour
- 1 **large green pepper**
- 1 **large red pepper**
- 3 **tablespoons olive or vegetable oil**
- 1 **clove garlic, minced**
- ¼ **cup dry red wine**
- 1 **tablespoon red wine vinegar**

1. Place chicken breast halves or pork between sheets of wax paper and pound firmly with a meat mallet or rolling pin until they are ¼-inch thick or thinner. Sprinkle with salt and pepper; dip in flour and pat briskly to remove the excess.
2. Halve peppers; seed; cut lengthwise into ½-inch strips.
3. Heat 2 tablespoons oil in large skillet. Add scaloppine and sauté until golden brown on both sides, about 5 minutes for chicken and 8 minutes for pork.
4. When meat is done, remove to platter; keep warm. Add remaining tablespoon of oil to skillet. Add pepper strips; sauté until tender. Add garlic and sauté 1 minute.
5. Stir in wine and vinegar, stirring to coat peppers with pan juices. Spoon peppers and juices over scaloppine.

SCALOPPINE NORMANDY

A tasty brandy cream sauce covers this scaloppine with sautéed apples.

Makes 4 servings.

- 2 **whole chicken breasts (about 14 ounces each), boned, skinned and halved**
  - OR: 4 **rib pork chops (each ½-inch thick), boned**
- ½ **teaspoon salt**
- ¼ **teaspoon pepper**
  Flour
- 2 **tart cooking apples, quartered, cored and sliced**
- 2 **tablespoons butter or margarine**
- 1 **tablespoon vegetable oil**
- 1 **small onion, minced (¼ cup)**
- ½ **cup chicken broth**
- ½ **cup light cream or half-and-half**
- 2 **tablespoons brandy**

1. Place chicken breast halves or pork between sheets of wax paper and pound firmly with a meat mallet or rolling pin until they are ¼-inch thick or thinner. Sprinkle with salt and pepper; dip in flour and pat briskly to remove the excess.
2. Sauté apple slices in butter in a large skillet just until tender. Remove apples to warmed platter; keep warm.
3. Heat oil with butter remaining in skillet. Add scaloppine and sauté until golden brown on both sides, about 5 minutes for chicken and 8 minutes for pork. Remove scaloppine to platter with apples.
4. Add onion to skillet and sauté until tender. Drain any fat remaining in pan. Add chicken broth and cook briskly until reduced by half. Add cream and brandy and continue to cook until sauce has thickened slightly. Pour over meat and apples.

SCALOPPINE IN MUSTARD SAUCE

These simple ingredients produce a delicious flavor.

Makes 4 servings.

- 2 **whole chicken breasts (about 14 ounces each), boned, skinned and halved**
  - OR: 4 **rib pork chops (each ½-inch thick), boned**
- ½ **teaspoon salt**
- ¼ **teaspoon pepper**
  Flour
- 1 **tablespoon vegetable oil**
- 1 **tablespoon butter or margarine**
- ½ **cup chicken broth**
- ¼ **cup dry sherry**
- 1 **to 2 tablespoons Dijon mustard**
- ¼ **cup light cream or half-and-half**

1. Place chicken breast halves or pork between sheets of wax paper and pound firmly with a meat mallet or rolling pin until they are ¼-inch thick or thinner. Sprinkle with salt and pepper; dip in flour and pat briskly to remove the excess.
2. Heat oil and butter in large skillet. Add scaloppine and sauté until meat is golden brown on both sides, about 5 minutes for chicken and 8 minutes for pork. Remove to warm platter; keep warm.
3. Drain any fat remaining in skillet. Add chicken broth, sherry and mustard to taste. Simmer, stirring to loosen brown bits from the bottom of the pan, until mixture is slightly reduced.
4. Add light cream and continue to simmer until sauce has thickened, about 2 to 3 minutes. Pour sauce over scaloppine.

Pictured opposite: Scaloppine with Orange Sauce, page 618

Scaloppine

SCALOPPINE AND ZUCCHINI AVGOLEMONO

The breaded scaloppine and sautéed zucchini are topped with a delicate lemon sauce.

Makes 4 servings.

- 2 **whole chicken breasts (about 14 ounces each), boned, skinned and halved**
  OR: **4 rib pork chops (each ½-inch thick), boned**
- ½ **teaspoon salt**
- ¼ **teaspoon pepper**
  Flour
- 1 **egg beaten with 2 tablespoons water**
- ⅔ **cup packaged bread crumbs**
- 3 **tablespoons olive oil**
- 1 **tablespoon butter or margarine**
- 1 **pound zucchini, cut in ½-inch slices**
- 1 **cup chicken broth**
- 3 **egg yolks**
- 2 **tablespoons lemon juice**
- ¼ **cup grated Parmesan cheese**

1. Place chicken breast halves or pork between sheets of wax paper and pound firmly with a meat mallet or rolling pin until they are ¼-inch thick or thinner. Sprinkle with salt and pepper; dip in flour and pat briskly to remove the excess. Dip the scaloppine in egg mixture, then coat evenly with bread crumbs.
2. Heat 2 tablespoons of the oil and the butter in large skillet. Add scaloppine and sauté until golden brown on both sides, about 5 minutes for chicken and 8 minutes for pork. Remove to platter; keep warm.
3. Heat remaining 1 tablespoon oil in skillet. Add zucchini slices in 1 layer; sauté, turning once, until tender. Remove and arrange evenly over scaloppine; keep warm in slow oven.
4. Drain all fat from skillet. Add broth; heat to boiling. Beat egg yolks and lemon juice in small bowl. Add hot broth, a little at a time, then return mixture to skillet; cook over very low heat, stirring constantly, until sauce thickens slightly. (Do not boil.) Pour over scaloppine and zucchini. Sprinkle with cheese.

SICILIAN SCALOPPINE

Bake at 400° for 10 minutes.
Makes 6 servings.

- 1 **eggplant (about 1 pound)**
- 1 **tablespoon salt**
- 3 **whole chicken breasts (about 14 ounces each), boned, skinned and halved**
  OR: **6 rib pork chops (each ½-inch thick), boned**
- ½ **teaspoon salt**
- ¼ **teaspoon pepper**
  Flour
- 1 **tablespoon butter or margarine**
- ⅓ **cup olive or vegetable oil**
- 1 **egg beaten with 2 tablespoons water**
- 1 **jar (about 16 ounces) spaghetti sauce**
- 1 **package (8 ounces) mozzarella cheese, cut into 6 slices**

1. Pare eggplant; cut off ends; cut into 6 slices. Sprinkle slices with salt and set aside for 30 minutes to drain. Rinse with water; pat dry with paper toweling.
2. Place chicken breast halves or pork between sheets of wax paper and pound firmly with a meat mallet or rolling pin until they are ¼-inch thick or thinner. Sprinkle with salt and pepper; dip in flour and pat briskly to remove the excess. Preheat oven to 400°.
3. Heat butter and 1 tablespoon of the oil in a large skillet. Sauté scaloppine until golden brown on both sides, about 5 minutes for chicken and 8 minutes for pork. Remove meat to paper toweling as it browns.
4. Coat eggplant slices with flour; dip in egg mixture. Heat remaining oil in skillet. Add eggplant; sauté until golden brown on both sides. Drain on paper toweling as slices are browned.
5. Pour half the spaghetti sauce in a shallow baking dish. Alternate slices of scaloppine, eggplant and mozzarella cheese, slightly overlapping until the bottom of the dish is covered with 1 layer. Drizzle top with remaining sauce.
6. Bake in a preheated hot oven (400°) for 10 minutes or until sauce is bubbly.

SCALOPPINE WITH LEMON ZEST

Makes 4 servings.

- 2 **whole chicken breasts (about 14 ounces each), boned, skinned and halved**
  OR: **4 rib pork chops (each ½-inch thick), boned**
- ½ **teaspoon salt**
- ¼ **teaspoon pepper**
  Flour
- 1 **lemon**
- 1 **tablespoon vegetable oil**
- 1 **tablespoon butter or margarine**
- ½ **teaspoon leaf rosemary, crumbled**
- 1 **large clove garlic, minced**
- ¼ **cup dry white wine**
- ½ **cup chicken broth**
- ½ **cup dairy sour cream**

1. Place chicken breast halves or pork between sheets of wax paper and pound firmly with a meat mallet or rolling pin until they are ¼-inch thick or thinner. Sprinkle with salt and pepper; dip in flour and pat briskly to remove the excess.
2. Remove rind from lemon (yellow part only) with vegetable parer. Stack strips on a chopping board and cut crosswise into fine julienne strips.
3. Heat oil and butter in large skillet. Sauté scaloppine until golden brown on both sides, about 5 minutes for chicken and 8 minutes for pork.
4. Sprinkle rosemary and garlic over scaloppine and shake the pan to distribute evenly for about 30 seconds. Add wine and chicken broth. Cook, uncovered, until the pan liquid has reduced a little.
5. Remove scaloppine to warm platter. Stir sour cream and half of the lemon rind into liquid in skillet. Heat over low heat, but do not boil. Pour sauce over scaloppine and sprinkle with remaining lemon rind.

SCALOPPINE WITH ORANGE SAUCE

Makes 4 servings.

- 2 **whole chicken breasts (about 14 ounces each), boned, skinned and halved**
  OR: **4 rib pork chops (each ½-inch thick), boned**
- 1 **teaspoon salt**

¼ teaspoon pepper
   Flour
2 large navel oranges
1 tablespoon olive oil
1 tablespoon butter or margarine
1 small onion, minced (¼ cup)
2 teaspoons tomato paste
1 cup chicken broth
2 tablespoons minced fresh
   parsley

1. Place chicken breast halves or pork between sheets of wax paper and pound firmly with a meat mallet or rolling pin until they are ¼-inch thick or thinner. Sprinkle with salt and pepper; dip in flour and pat briskly to remove excess.

2. Grate the rind of 1 orange; reserve. Cut off all remaining rind and white from both oranges. Cut each in half lengthwise, then cut crosswise into ½-inch slices.

3. Heat oil and butter in large skillet. Add scaloppine and sauté until golden on both sides, about 5 minutes for chicken and 8 minutes for pork. Remove to platter; keep warm.

4. Add onion to skillet; sauté until soft but not brown, about 3 minutes. Stir in tomato paste, chicken broth and rind. Return scaloppine to pan; cover; simmer until tender, about 5 minutes for chicken and 8 minutes for pork.

5. When scaloppine is tender, remove to warm platter. Add orange slices to sauce in skillet and heat through. Spoon over scaloppine. Sprinkle with parsley. Garnish with parsley sprigs, if you wish.

— • • • —

SCAMPI In the United States, the word ''scampi'' refers to a cooked dish of shrimp in a garlic butter sauce. Originally, it was an Italian term for a Mediterranean crustacean which grows up to 6 inches in length.

The true *scampo* (*scampi* is plural) resembles a tiny lobster. Only the tail portion has the edible meat. The Italian scampo is also called Dublin Bay prawn, langoustine, Danish lobster or lobsterette. See also **SHRIMP.**

SCONE Triangular or diamond-shaped biscuit-like tea cake of Scottish origin. Pronounced SKAHN, it is baked on a griddle or in a hot oven.

GRIDDLE SCONES
Makes 8 scones.
1½ cups lightly spooned
     all-purpose flour
½ teaspoon salt
½ teaspoon baking soda
½ teaspoon cream of tartar
¼ cup sugar
¼ cup (½ stick) butter or
     margarine
1 egg
¼ cup buttermilk

1. Sift the flour, salt, baking soda, cream of tartar and sugar into a medium-size bowl. Cut in the butter with a pastry blender until mixture forms crumbs.

2. Beat the egg with the buttermilk in a small bowl and add to the flour mixture, stirring to make a soft dough. Turn dough onto a floured surface and roll or pat out into a ½-inch-thick round. Cut into 8 triangles.

3. Heat griddle over low to medium heat; sprinkle lightly with flour. Bake triangles about 5 minutes or until the underside is golden brown; turn over and finish baking 4 to 5 minutes longer. Split; spread with butter and jam.

Fruit Scones: Follow recipe for Griddle Scones, adding ¼ teaspoon ground cinnamon with flour, and ½ cup raisins with buttermilk.

Cheese Scones: Follow recipe for Griddle Scones but using only 2 tablespoons sugar and adding ¼ teaspoon pepper, ¼ teaspoon dry mustard, and ¼ to ½ cup shredded Cheddar cheese to dry ingredients.

Whole Wheat Scones: Follow recipe for Griddle Scones but using ¾ cup whole wheat flour and ¾ cup all-purpose flour in place of all white flour. Increase baking soda to 1 teaspoon.

— • • • —

SCRAPPLE A loaf-shaped, firm cornmeal mush and pork mixture that is sliced and fried for a breakfast or supper dish. It was created by early German settlers in Pennsylvania to use up the bits and pieces of pork after butchering hogs. Commercially-made scrapple can be purchased from the refrigerated meat or dairy case in the supermarket.

SCROD A fish marketing term used for young cod or haddock weighing 1½ to 2½ pounds.

SEAFOOD Any marine fish or shellfish used for food. See also **FISH** and specific kinds of fish or shellfish.

SEA URCHIN Resembling a large pin cushion, the sea urchin is a seafood delicacy. A menace to swimmers, sea urchins cling to rocks along shallow shores, in creeks, tidal pools and on reefs. It is the cream- to orange-colored roe that is eaten.

Though there are several hundred species of edible urchins worldwide, their perishability limits them to coastal markets. Generally they can be found from August to April.

To Prepare: Cut the mouth or underside of the shell with scissors and discard the viscera. The roe is attached to the top side of the shell. Scoop out with a spoon onto sliced crusty French bread. Drizzle with lemon juice and enjoy with white wine. Allow 6 to 12 urchins to provide enough roe for a serving.

SELTZER A mineral water originating from Nieder Selters in the Wiesbaden district of Germany. The water is now artificially prepared and bottled. It contains a great deal of carbon dioxide.

SEMOLINA The pale, golden heart or endosperm of durum wheat. It may be finely milled into flour which is used in making pasta products, or granular, which is called couscous.

SESAME SEEDS The tiny creamy-white or black seeds of an aromatic, herbaceous plant. Sesame grows to a height of 2 to 4 feet in tropical and subtropical areas. Native to India, the plant is cultivated both in India and China. The seeds are used whole, toasted, ground or pressed to extract the oil. Not only are the seeds widely used in Far Eastern cooking, sesame is also used in the Middle East. The seeds are ground into a paste and spread on bread. Sesame paste is available in health food and specialty food stores.

Sesame seeds were brought to America by African slaves who called them "benne seeds." They were planted in the South and are popular in Southern cooking.

White sesame seeds are widely available; black sesame seeds are sold in specialty food stores. Use them to add crunch to salads, in candies and on breads. Sesame oil found in Oriental markets is extracted from toasted white sesame seeds and has a nutty flavor. Sesame oil from un-toasted sesame seeds available in health-food stores is bland. Sesame oil is best used as a condiment or salad dressing oil rather than for cooking. Store in the refrigerator.

To toast white sesame seeds, place seeds in a skillet or saucepan. Heat until they begin to turn golden, shaking pan frequently. Remove from heat and cool before storing. See also **BENNE.**

SESAME CHICKEN WINGS

Miniature "drumsticks" in a cream and crumb coating "fry" with ease in the oven. Delicious hot or cold.

Bake at 375° for 40 minutes.
Makes about 36 appetizers.

- **3 pounds chicken wings (about 18)**
- **2 tablespoons toasted sesame seeds***
- **¾ cup packaged bread crumbs**
- **1 teaspoon paprika**
- **½ teaspoon salt**
- **⅓ cup heavy cream**
- **½ cup (1 stick) butter**
  Bottled duck sauce

1. Remove tips of chicken wings; save for making soup. Cut each wing into two sections.
2. Combine sesame seeds, bread crumbs, paprika and salt in shallow dish.

3. Dip chicken pieces in cream, using brush to coat completely; roll in crumb mixture. Refrigerate 1 hour.
4. Place butter in a 13×9×2-inch baking pan. Melt in oven while oven preheats to 375°. Remove from oven; turn chicken pieces in butter to coat completely.
5. Bake in a moderate oven (375°) for 40 minutes. Serve with duck sauce.
*Shake sesame seeds in small skillet over low heat until golden.

SESAME CRUNCH

These candies are easy to make using honey, sesame seeds and brown sugar.

Makes 1 pound (52 pieces).

- **2 cups sesame seeds (about 12 ounces)**
- **½ cup honey**
- **½ cup firmly packed light brown sugar**
- **½ teaspoon ground ginger**
- **½ teaspoon ground cinnamon**
- **¼ teaspoon salt**

1. Heat sesame seeds in a large skillet over medium heat until lightly browned, stirring frequently. Remove to a bowl; wipe skillet clean.
2. Combine honey, sugar, ginger, cinnamon and salt in same skillet. Heat to boiling over medium heat, stirring constantly. Boil 2 minutes.
3. Butter or coat a 10¾×7-inch pan with vegetable cooking spray. Stir seeds into syrup; pour into pan. Spread candy to an even layer with buttered metal spatula. Cool on wire rack 15 minutes. Lift out of pan to board.
4. Cut candy with a large knife into 4 lengthwise strips. Cut each strip crosswise into thirteen ¾-inch pieces. When pieces are firm, wrap individually in plastic wrap or store in single layer in airtight container.

SESAME BROCCOLI

Makes 8 servings.

- **1 bunch broccoli (about 2 pounds)**
- **¼ cup (½ stick) butter**
- **¼ cup water**
- **1 tablespoon soy sauce**
- **1 cup thinly sliced celery**
- **1 can (8 ounces) water chestnuts, drained and sliced**
- **1 tablespoon sesame seeds**

1. Trim outer leaves and tough ends from broccoli. Cut stalks and flowerets into 2-inch lengths, then slice lengthwise.
2. Combine butter, water and soy sauce in large skillet; bring to boiling. Stir in the broccoli, celery and water chestnuts; bring to boiling again; cover. Steam 10 minutes or just until broccoli is crisply tender.
3. While broccoli cooks, heat sesame seeds in a small, heavy skillet over low heat, shaking pan constantly, just until lightly toasted; stir into broccoli mixture. Spoon into a heated serving bowl. Serve with more soy sauce to sprinkle over top.

———————— •••• ————————

SHAD Related to herring, shad is found in the north Atlantic, in the Mediterranean and off the Pacific coast. Like salmon, shad is caught when it runs up river to spawn. As a result, the season for shad begins in December in the south, to late May in the north. Shad is a bony fish with a pink, sweet-tasting flesh. The roe of the female shad is highly prized by gourmets.

Shad is marketed fresh, weighing from 1½ to 8 pounds, and in fillets with the skin left on because the flesh is so delicate it may fall apart after cooking without the skin. Shad can be broiled, grilled, baked or pan-fried.

SHALLOT Often called "the onion of the epicure," shallots are small, rosy-pink bulbs closely resembling cloves of garlic. The cloves are covered with a yellowish-brown skin. Shallots are mild-flavored. Use them for seasoning delicately flavored foods since they themselves are delicate.

Fresh shallots, available in spring in some markets, have green leaves similar to green onions. Fresh shallots can be eaten raw as a relish or in salads, or cut up and cooked as a seasoning. Dried shallots are simply the bulbs without the leaves, which are allowed to shrivel and die. Dried shallots are available during the fall months. Store them in a cool, dry place.

SHELLFISH Divided into two categories, shellfish are either mollusks or crustaceans. Mollusks have a soft body and are partially or wholly enclosed in a single or two-part shell. Single-shelled (univalve) mollusks include the abalone, conch and periwinkle. Two-part, shelled (bivalve) mollusks are clams, mussels, oysters and scallops. Crustaceans have thin shells and segmented bodies. They include lobsters, crabs and shrimp.

In general, shellfish are low in calories, contain high-quality protein and are a good source of vitamins and minerals.

Uncooked fresh shellfish should be purchased live. Bivalve mollusks, except for scallops, should be tightly closed. Shucked mollusks should be fresh-smelling and plump with little or no liquor. Crabs and lobsters should be lively when picked up.

Keep fresh shellfish loosely wrapped and refrigerated. Cook or use shellfish within 1 day after purchase.

See also specific kinds of shellfish.

SHERBET Along with ice cream, sherbet is a favorite frozen dessert. Sherbet is made of a fruit puree or juice, a sweetener, water and milk. Egg white or gelatin is sometimes added. Some people think of sherbet and ice as the same but they differ. Ice is considered a nondairy product because it's made of fruit or juice, a sweetener and water.

PEACHY SHERBET

No need to wait for the peach season to make this sherbet. Frozen sliced peaches work perfectly.

Makes 2 quarts.

- **2 packages (10 or 12 ounces each) frozen sliced peaches, slightly thawed**
- **1 can (14 ounces) sweetened condensed milk**
- **¼ cup lemon juice**
- **¼ teaspoon almond extract**
- **2 cups milk**
- **1 envelope unflavored gelatin**

1. Puree peaches, half at a time, in container of electric blender or put through a food mill. Combine peach puree with sweetened condensed milk, lemon juice and almond extract.
2. Combine milk and gelatin in a small saucepan. Heat and stir over low heat until gelatin is dissolved, about 5 minutes; cool. Combine with puree mixture.
3. Pour into a 13 × 9 × 2-inch pan, set in the freezer and freeze 2 hours or until mushy-firm. Break up semi-frozen mixture; beat in a chilled large bowl with electric mixer until fluffy.
4. Pack in freezer containers and store in the freezer. Allow the sherbet to soften somewhat before serving.

STRAWBERRY SHERBET

A delightfully smooth, fresh berry frozen dessert, this sherbet can be made in either an ice cream freezer or in the freezer section of refrigerator.

Makes about 1 quart.

- **1 cup sugar**
- **¼ cup light corn syrup**
- **¾ cup water**
- **½ cup orange juice**
- **¼ cup lemon juice**
- **2 pints strawberries
  OR: 1 bag (20 ounces) frozen unsweetened strawberries, thawed**

For Refrigerator-Freezer Method:
- **2 egg whites**
- **2 tablespoons sugar**

Method for Ice Cream Freezer:
1. Combine sugar, syrup and water in small saucepan; bring to boiling, stirring constantly, until sugar is dissolved. Cook 5 minutes over low heat. Remove from heat; stir in orange and lemon juices; cool completely.
2. Wash and hull strawberries; puree in container of electric blender, adding about ½ cup of the sugar syrup. Stir in the remaining syrup.
3. Pour mixture into freezer can; adjust dasher and top. Freeze, using recommended amounts of ice and salt and following manufacturer's directions. Spoon mixture into plastic containers; cover. Return to freezer until firm.

Method for Refrigerator-Freezer:
Before you begin, make sure freezer section will maintain 0°.
3. Follow recipe through Step 2. Pour strawberry mixture into a 9 × 9 × 2-inch pan. Place in freezer with the pan touching one of the freezing surfaces. Freeze mixture, stirring several times for even freezing, until frozen to a mush, about 4 hours.
4. Beat 2 egg whites until foamy-white in a small bowl. Beat in 2 tablespoons of sugar slowly until meringue forms soft peaks.
5. Break up frozen mixture and spoon into chilled large bowl. Beat with electric mixer until very smooth. Fold in meringue, working quickly so mixture does not melt. Spoon into plastic containers; cover. Return to freezer for at least 6 hours or until firm.

———— ●●● ————

SHERRY An excellent before- or after-dinner drink, sherry is a fortified wine made from grapes. The original wine is made in Jerez, Spain, but sherries are also made in the United States. Sherry is considered a white wine although its color varies from a pale yellow to a rich brown. The word sherry is derived from "xeres" which was the early name of Jerez.

Sherry is a blend of wines from many harvests. There is a variety of blends to choose from—Manzanilla, Fino, Amontillado, Oloroso and Cream. The very dry Manzanillas and dry Finos are pale yellow. Serve them well chilled before a meal. The amber, moderately dry Amontillado is the wine for those who prefer a fuller-bodied, less dry drink before dinner. Oloroso is dark brownish in color and slightly sweet. It can be served with appetizers or as a dessert wine. Cream sherry is rich, sweet and dark. It's a distinctive wine with which to finish a meal.

Use the dry sherries in stir-fried dishes, seafood sauces and soups. Use the sweet sherries to flavor desserts.

SHERRIED CHICKEN LIVERS

This canapé spread is excellent on melba toast or pumpernickel bread rounds.

Makes 8 servings.

- 1 large onion, chopped (1 cup)
- 2 tablespoons butter or margarine
- 1 pound chicken livers, trimmed and halved
- ⅔ cup dry sherry
- 3 tablespoons brandy
- 1 teaspoon salt
- ¼ teaspoon pepper
  Boston lettuce

1. Sauté onion in butter in a large skillet until soft. Stir in livers and sherry. Simmer, uncovered, 20 minutes.
2. Place half the mixture in container of electric blender. Cover. Whirl until smooth; remove to a small bowl. Repeat with remaining mixture. Stir in brandy, salt and pepper. Cover and chill.
3. To serve: Pipe or spoon about ¼ cup of the mixture onto a leaf of lettuce for each serving. Garnish with thin slivers of truffle, cocktail onions, thin tomato slices and parsley, if you wish.

FRUIT MOLDED IN SHERRY JELLY

This shimmering jewel of a gelatin dessert is refreshing and cool.

Makes 8 servings.

- 2 envelopes unflavored gelatin
- 1 cup water
- ¾ cup medium dry sherry
- 1 can (12 ounces) peach nectar
- ¼ cup sugar
- 3 large peaches
- 1 large banana
- ½ pint strawberries
- 1 cup heavy cream

1. Sprinkle gelatin over water in a medium-size saucepan. Let stand 5 minutes to soften. Heat saucepan over low heat until gelatin dissolves. Remove from heat; stir in sherry, nectar and sugar. Chill mixture until syrupy or it has consistency of unbeaten egg whites, about 1 hour.
2. Dip peaches into boiling water 30 seconds, then into ice water 1 minute. Peel, halve, pit and slice. Peel and slice banana; wash, hull and quarter strawberries.
3. Pour about ½-inch layer of gelatin in bottom of a 6-cup mold. Leave remaining gelatin at room temperature. Set mold in bowl of ice and water. Swirl mold until gelatin is thickened and coats bottom of mold. Arrange pieces of fruit against bottom and halfway up side of mold. Leave mold in ice water until fruit is set in gelatin.
4. Add a third of remaining gelatin to mold. Add a third of remaining fruit. Repeat layering until mold is filled. Chill mold 4 hours or overnight.
5. To serve: Unmold by dipping mold in warm water, then inverting onto platter. Beat cream until soft peaks form; serve with mold. Garnish with additional peach slices and sprigs of mint, if you wish.

———————— ●●● ————————

SHISH KEBOB Originally, a dish of lamb skewered with other foods and grilled or broiled. The word is derived from the Turkish *shish,* skewered, and *kebap,* roast meat. It was a convenient method of cooking food over a fire devised by the nomadic people of the Near East. Nowadays, any type of meat, poultry or even seafood is skewered. See also **KABOB.**

SHISH KEBOB

Makes 6 servings.

- 1 medium-size onion, sliced
- 3 cloves garlic, crushed
- 1 cup chopped celery
- ¼ teaspoon cumin seeds
- 1 cup red wine vinegar
- 1 cup lemon juice
- ½ cup vegetable oil
- 1 teaspoon salt
- ¼ teaspoon pepper
- ½ leg of lamb (butt end), about 2½ pounds
- 2 large onions, cut in 1½-inch pieces
- 6 medium-size mushroom caps
- 6 green peppers, halved, seeded and quartered
  Hot cooked rice

1. Combine sliced onion, garlic, celery, cumin, vinegar, lemon juice, oil, salt and pepper in a medium-size bowl.
2. Bone the lamb; cut meat into 1-inch cubes. Place in a glass or ceramic dish. Pour marinade over lamb; cover; refrigerate 24 hours.
3. Blanch onion pieces in boiling water 5 minutes; drain.
4. Thread a mushroom, pepper and onion piece on long skewers alternately with pieces of the marinated lamb. Place skewers on rack over broiler pan.
5. Broil kebobs 4 inches from heat for 5 minutes. Turn; baste with marinade; broil 5 minutes; turn; broil 5 minutes longer. Serve kebobs on rice.

———————— ●●● ————————

SHORTBREAD This rich, pastry-like firm cookie was traditionally served at Hogmanay, the Scottish New Year's Day. Shortbread has been made in Scotland for four centuries. It is made of flour, sugar and butter, formed into a round patty, scored, the edges crimped, and baked until dry in a slow oven. It is then broken into pieces.

SHORTBREAD

Bake at 325° for 25 minutes.
Makes 2 dozen cookies.

- 1 cup (2 sticks) butter, softened
- ½ cup sugar
- 2½ cups *sifted* all-purpose flour

1. Preheat oven to 325°. Beat butter and sugar in a large bowl until creamy and smooth. Work in flour with a wooden spoon until a stiff dough forms.
2. Divide dough into 3 parts. Working with one part at a time, roll out to about a 5-inch circle on an ungreased cookie sheet. Score circle with knife into 8 equal wedges. Pierce dough along the score lines with tines of fork. Make sure the tines go through the entire thickness to facilitate breaking later. Press back of fork around edge of cookie to decorate. Repeat with remaining dough.
3. Bake in a preheated slow oven (325°) for 25 minutes or until cookies are faintly golden brown. They

should be quite pale.

4. Remove from oven to wire rack. While still warm, break along score lines. Remove cookies to racks to cool. Store in covered containers.

●●●

SHORTCAKE An original American favorite, shortcake with strawberries can only be topped by whipped cream. Although the shortcake can be a sponge cake baked in a MaryAnne shape, the classic is a biscuitlike cake.

OLD-FASHIONED STRAWBERRY SHORTCAKE

Bake at 450° for 15 minutes.
Makes 6 servings.

 2 cups *sifted* all-purpose flour
 1 tablespoon sugar
 3 teaspoons baking powder
 ¼ teaspoon salt
   Pinch ground nutmeg
 ½ cup (1 stick) butter or margarine, chilled
 1 egg
 ⅔ cups heavy cream
 2 pints strawberries
 1 tablespoon sugar

1. Preheat oven to 450°.
2. Combine flour, sugar, baking powder, salt and nutmeg in a medium-size bowl. Cut in butter with a pastry blender or two knives until mixture forms coarse crumbs. Stir in egg and ⅔ cup of the heavy cream until mixture comes together in a ball. Pat into a lightly greased and floured 8-inch round layer-cake pan.
3. Bake in a preheated very hot oven (450°) for 15 minutes or until lightly browned. Remove from pan and place on a wire rack to cool slightly.
4. Whip remaining 1 cup cream in a small bowl. Cut cake in half horizontally while cake is still warm. Wash and hull berries. Crush enough to make 1 cup. Stir in 1 tablespoon sugar. Slice remaining berries. Spread bottom layer with crushed berries, half of the whipped cream and some of the sliced berries. Add top layer of cake and spread with remaining cream. Arrange berries on top and serve immediately.

●●●

SHORTENING Any fat, either solid or liquid, that helps tenderize baked goods by "shortening" the strands of gluten in the batter or dough. The baked product is flaky and thus considered tender. The fats most often used are vegetable shortening, lard, butter, margarine and vegetable oil.

SHRIMP A crustacean popular the world over and found in both salt and fresh waters. Shrimp are found all around the coasts of North America including Alaska. Shrimp are commercially harvested along the Gulf Coast states and Alaska, Mexico, and as far away as Brazil. Presently, the "farming" of shrimp is in the experimental stages. Shrimp have been successfully raised to marketable sizes in controlled waters but they are still too expensive to produce.

Most of the shrimp marketed are frozen. Shrimp deteriorate quickly when removed from the water and must be frozen to preserve them. When shrimp are caught, their heads and most of their bodies are discarded. Only the abdomens and tails of shrimp are marketed. Thus, what is marketed for shrimp is the segmented abdomen with its five sets of swimming paddles and the tail fin. Fresh shrimp, with head, legs and all, can be found in local fish markets.

Shrimp not only vary in size but in color and name. The difference in names depends on local custom. In the Far East, shrimp are called prawns. Around the Mediterranean Sea, shrimp are called prawns and scampi. In the United States, large shrimp are called prawns; scampi refers to a prepared shrimp dish. Correctly, freshwater species should be called prawns, marine or saltwater species should be called shrimp, and a lobsterette is a scampo, the singular form of scampi. Rock shrimp tails have recently been introduced to fish markets. Rock shrimp are caught in the water off Florida and Mexico. Rock shrimp look more like a tiny lobster than any of its relatives. Only the meat-containing tails are marketed.

Shrimp is a versatile seafood, being equally elegant in soups and appetizers, served hot or cold, sweet and sour or simply plain. They are high in protein and low in fat. A 3½-ounce raw portion contains only 91 calories. They generally contain the highest amount of iodine among the crustaceans. They are a good source of vitamins and minerals.

Buying and Storing: Raw shrimp is marketed shelled fresh or frozen, or breaded and uncooked. Although raw shrimp is sold by the pound, it helps to know the number of shrimp or "count" per pound. *Jumbo* or *extra large* shrimp contain up to 20 per pound; *large* shrimp contain 21 to 30 per pound; *medium* contain 31 to 40 per pound; *small* shrimp contain any number over 40 per pound. How much shrimp to buy depends on how they will be served. For appetizers, allow 6 medium to large shrimp for a serving. Generally, 1 pound of *unshelled* shrimp yields ½ pound of cooked, shelled meat, or about 2 servings. One pound of *shelled* shrimp yields 3 servings. Cooked shrimp is marketed fresh, canned and frozen.

To Prepare: To shell shrimp, slip thumb under shell at cut end of shrimp. Lift off several segments. Pull shrimp out from rest of shell and tail segment. To devein, cut along outside curve of shrimp ⅛ inch deep with a sharp knife. Lift out the black vein. Wash shrimp under water. Pat dry with paper toweling. To butterfly a shrimp, shell the shrimp but leave the last segment and tail in place. With small knife, cut shrimp along the inner curve down to the last segment without cutting through the shrimp. Open shrimp and rinse under running cold water to remove vein. Pat dry with paper toweling.

To Cook: Place raw shelled or unshelled shrimp in a saucepan or skillet with boiling water to cover. Return water to boiling. Simmer shrimp just until firm, from 1 to 3 minutes. Drain and cool, if using for appetizer or a salad. Shrimp can also be broiled, fried, stir-fried or baked.

Shrimp

SHRIMP PÂTÉ CANAPÉS

Makes 6 to 7 dozen.

- 1½ **pounds cooked, shelled and deveined shrimp**
- 2 **tablespoons lemon juice**
- 2 **tablespoons prepared horseradish**
- ¼ **cup chili sauce**
- 1 **jar (6 ounces) tartar sauce**
- 1 **teaspoon salt**
- 4 **large cucumbers**
  - OR: **Crackers or slices of toast**
- 1 **jar (4 ounces) red caviar**

1. Place shrimp, lemon juice, horseradish, chili sauce, tartar sauce and salt in container of electric blender; whirl until smooth; cover and chill.
2. Cut unpeeled cucumbers into ¼-inch diagonal slices; chill.
3. When ready to serve, spread cucumber with pâté. Top each with a tiny spoonful of red caviar.

PICKLED SHRIMP

Makes about 40.

- 3 **cups water**
- ¼ **cup mixed pickling spice (tied in cheesecloth bag)**
- ¼ **cup chopped celery leaves**
- 2½ **teaspoons salt**
- 2 **packages (1 pound each) frozen shrimp, shelled and deveined**
- 1 **medium-size onion, sliced and separated into rings**
- 6 **bay leaves**
- 1 **cup olive or vegetable oil**
- ⅔ **cup tarragon or white wine vinegar**
- 1 **teaspoon celery seeds**
- 2 **tablespoons drained capers Lemon wedges**

1. Combine water, pickling spice, celery leaves and 1¼ teaspoons of the salt in a large saucepan. Bring to boiling; add shrimp. Cook following time on label directions; drain.
2. Transfer shrimp to a large shallow non-metal dish. Add onion and bay leaves.
3. Beat oil, vinegar, celery seeds and remaining salt in a small bowl; add capers; pour over shrimp; toss to coat. Cover with plastic wrap; refrigerate. Let marinate 2 days. (It will keep for a week.)

4. To serve: Drain shrimp with capers and place in glass bowl. Place this bowl in a larger bowl of crushed ice. Garnish with lemon wedges. Serve with wooden picks.

SHRIMP SCAMPI

Makes 4 servings.

- 1 **pound large raw shrimp (see Note)**
- ½ **cup (1 stick) butter or margarine**
- ¼ **cup olive or vegetable oil**
- 1 **tablespoon finely chopped garlic**

1. Cut shrimp down the back lengthwise with kitchen shears, being careful not to cut through the shrimp. With shells intact, remove black vein; rinse and pat dry.
2. Melt butter with oil in a large skillet. Add garlic; cook until garlic just begins to brown.
3. Add shrimp; sauté, shaking skillet and stirring, 2 to 3 minutes or just until shrimp is pink and firm. Garnish with chopped parsley and lemon wedges, if you wish.
Note: If using frozen, shelled, deveined shrimp, defrost, then begin recipe at Step 2.

SHRIMP AND CLAM SOUP

Makes 8 servings.

- ½ **cup frozen chopped onion**
- ½ **cup frozen chopped green pepper**
- 2 **cloves garlic, crushed**
- 1 **tablespoon vegetable oil**
- 1 **teaspoon salt**
- ½ **teaspoon pepper**
- 1 **can (35 ounces) plum tomatoes**
- 2 **bottles (8 ounces each) clam juice**
- 1 **cup dry white wine**
- 1 **package (1 pound) frozen shelled and deveined shrimp**
- 1 **can (8 ounces) minced clams with juice**
- 1½ **teaspoons grated lemon rind**
- ¼ **cup finely chopped fresh parsley**

1. Sauté onion, green pepper and garlic in oil in a large saucepan until soft and tender. Add salt and pepper.
2. Stir in tomatoes, clam juice and

wine. Bring to boiling; lower heat. Simmer 5 minutes. Set aside until 10 minutes before serving. Reheat, add shrimp and simmer until they are tender, about 5 minutes.
3. Add clams and their juice, lemon rind and parsley; heat until thoroughly hot. (Do not boil.)

POTTED SHRIMP BUTTER

Makes about ¾ cup.

- 1 **package (7 ounces) frozen shelled and deveined shrimp**
- ½ **cup (1 stick) butter**
- 1 **clove garlic, minced**
- 2 **tablespoons finely chopped fresh parsley**
- 1 **tablespoon finely chopped onion**
- 1 **teaspoon grated lemon rind**
- ½ **teaspoon salt**
- ⅛ **teaspoon pepper**

1. Cook shrimp following package directions; drain; cool; chop finely.
2. Beat butter in a small bowl with electric mixer. Stir in shrimp, garlic, parsley, onion, lemon rind, salt and pepper. Spoon into crock; cover. Refrigerate several hours. Allow to soften slightly before serving. Serve with crackers, if you wish.

SHRIMP BISQUE

Makes 8 servings.

- ½ **cup (1 stick) butter**
- 1 **medium-size carrot, thinly sliced**
- 1 **small onion, chopped (¼ cup)**
- 1 **bay leaf**
- ¼ **teaspoon leaf thyme, crumbled**
- ½ **cup dry white wine**
- ¾ **pound raw shrimp, shelled and deveined**
- ⅓ **cup all-purpose flour**
- ½ **teaspoon salt**
- 2 **to 3 teaspoons paprika**
- 3 **cups milk**
- 2 **cups half-and-half Fresh dill sprigs**

1. Melt 2 tablespoons of the butter in a large saucepan. Sauté carrot and onion until tender, about 3 minutes. Add bay leaf, thyme, wine and shrimp. Cook just until shrimp turn pink, about 3 minutes. Drain shrimp

into a bowl, reserving liquid.

2. Melt remaining 6 tablespoons butter in same saucepan; stir in flour. Cook, stirring constantly, until bubbly. Add reserved shrimp liquid to saucepan along with salt, paprika and milk. Cook, stirring constantly, until mixture thickens.

3. Reserve 8 whole shrimp; coarsely chop remainder. Add chopped shrimp and vegetables with half-and-half to saucepan; heat thoroughly. Garnish with reserved whole shrimp and fresh dill.

BUTTERFLIED COCONUT SHRIMP

Makes about 24 appetizers.

- **1 pound large raw shrimp**
  Vegetable oil for frying
- **¼ cup all-purpose flour**
- **½ teaspoon salt**
- **½ teaspoon dry mustard**
- **1 egg**
- **2 tablespoons cream or milk**
- **¾ cup flaked coconut**
- **⅓ cup packaged bread crumbs**
  Chinese Mustard Sauce *(recipe follows)*

1. Shell and devein shrimp, leaving tails on. Slit shrimp with sharp knife along curved side, cutting almost through. Place on paper toweling.

2. Pour oil into a medium-size saucepan to a depth of 2 inches. Heat to 350° on deep-fat frying thermometer.

3. While oil is heating, combine flour, salt and dry mustard in one small bowl; beat egg and cream in second small bowl. In third bowl, combine coconut and bread crumbs.

4. Dip shrimp in flour mixture, then in egg-cream mixture, then in coconut-crumb mixture, coating well. Refrigerate until ready to cook.

5. When oil is hot, fry shrimp, a few at a time, turning once, for 2 minutes or until golden. Remove with slotted spoon and drain on paper toweling. Keep warm in oven. Serve with Chinese Mustard Sauce and bottled duck sauce, if you wish.

Chinese Mustard Sauce: Mix ⅓ cup dry mustard with 1 tablespoon honey, 2 teaspoons vinegar and ¼ cup cold water until well blended. Keep refrigerated. Makes about ⅓ cup.

CREAMY SHRIMP DIP

Makes 2⅓ cups.

- **1 cup mayonnaise**
- **½ cup dairy sour cream**
- **2 tablespoons catsup**
- **2 tablespoons minced onion**
- **1 tablespoon dry sherry (optional)**
- **½ teaspoon Worcestershire sauce**
- **⅛ teaspoon cayenne**
- **1 package (6 ounces) frozen cooked tiny shrimp, thawed according to package directions and drained**

1. Blend mayonnaise, sour cream, catsup, onion, sherry, Worcestershire and cayenne in a medium-size bowl. Add shrimp and mix well.

2. Spoon into a serving bowl and serve at once or cover and refrigerate up to 5 hours before serving.

SHRIMP ON CHINESE CABBAGE

Makes 4 servings.

- **1 pound raw shrimp, shelled and deveined**
  OR: 1 package (1 pound) frozen shelled and deveined shrimp, thawed
- **1 small head Chinese celery cabbage**
- **3 green onions**
- **¼ cup water**
- **1 tablespoon cornstarch**
- **3 tablespoons vegetable oil**
- **½ teaspoon salt**
- **½ teaspoon sugar**
- **1 tablespoon soy sauce**
- **1 clove garlic, minced**
- **2 tablespoons dry sherry**
- **4 to 6 dried small whole red peppers**
- **½ cup unsalted shelled roasted peanuts**

1. Rinse shrimp; pat dry with paper toweling. Cut cabbage into 1 × 2-inch pieces. (You should have about 8 cups.) Cut onions into 1-inch lengths. Mix water and cornstarch in 1-cup measure.

2. Heat large deep skillet, Dutch oven or wok over high heat. Add 1 tablespoon of the oil; swirl to coat bottom and side. Add cabbage; stir-fry until coated with oil. Add salt, sugar and

soy sauce. Stir-fry until just tender-crisp. Restir cornstarch mixture; remove 1 tablespoon and add to cabbage. Stir until juices are thickened. Remove cabbage to platter; keep warm.

3. Reheat pan with remaining oil. Add shrimp and garlic. Stir-fry just until shrimp turn firm and pink. Add sherry and peppers. Stir-fry to loosen browned bits in pan. Restir cornstarch mixture; pour over shrimp. Cook until sauce is thick and coats shrimp. Stir in green onions and peanuts. Taste for salt; add, if needed. Spoon shrimp over cabbage. Serve with hot fluffy rice, if you wish.

SHRIMP, EGG AND CUCUMBER SALAD

Makes 4 servings.

- **1 package (1 pound) frozen, shelled and deveined shrimp**
- **1 egg**
- **4 teaspoons lemon juice**
- **1 teaspoon salt**
- **¾ to 1 teaspoon curry powder**
- **⅓ cup peanut oil**
- **⅓ cup olive oil**
- **2 large cucumbers**
- **4 hard-cooked eggs**
- **1 head Boston lettuce, torn into pieces**
- **2 to 4 tablespoons light cream or milk**

1. Cook shrimp following label directions; cool; refrigerate.

2. Combine egg, lemon juice, ½ teaspoon of the salt and curry powder in container of electric blender. Cover. Whirl 1 minute. Combine peanut and olive oils in a cup. Slowly add oil in a thin stream, while blender is running, until mixture is smooth. Chill dressing.

3. Pare cucumbers and halve lengthwise. Scoop out seeds with a teaspoon or melon ball cutter; cut into ¼-inch slices. Sprinkle slices with remaining ½ teaspoon salt; refrigerate.

4. Peel eggs; slice. Arrange shrimp and eggs on a lettuce-lined platter. Ring with cucumbers.

5. Thin dressing with cream to a pouring consistency; drizzle over salad.

SHRIMP CURRY

A delightful, not-too-hot curry that is colorful and unusual.

Makes 6 servings.

- **2 tablespoons butter or margarine**
- **1 tablespoon vegetable oil**
- **1 cup frozen chopped onion**
- **4 teaspoons curry powder**
- **1 can condensed chicken broth**
- **½ teaspoon salt**
- **1 package (1½ pounds) frozen shelled and deveined shrimp**
- **2 tablespoons cornstarch**
- **½ teaspoon ground ginger**
- **2 tablespoons water**
- **1 tablespoon lime juice**
- **1 tomato, cut into wedges**
- **1 cup shredded lettuce**
  Hot cooked rice

1. Heat butter and oil in large skillet; sauté onion until soft, about 5 minutes. Stir in curry powder; cook, stirring constantly, 2 minutes longer. Add chicken broth, salt and shrimp. Bring to boiling; simmer for 6 minutes.

2. Blend cornstarch, ginger, water and lime juice in a small bowl. Stir into shrimp mixture; continue cooking and stirring until mixture thickens and bubbles 1 minute. Stir in tomato wedges and shredded lettuce. Cover; simmer 3 minutes longer or until tomatoes are hot, but still firm. Serve over hot cooked rice. Serve with chutney, shredded coconut and peanuts, if you wish.

— • • • —

SKILLET COOKERY A skillet or frypan is a shallow, flat-bottomed metal pan with a long handle. It is designed for cooking foods quickly in a small amount of fat. A good skillet should be made of a metal that heats quickly and cooks the food evenly. Cast iron was one of the first materials used to make cooking utensils. The metal heats uniformly with no hot spots and holds heat well. It is inexpensive and darkens with age. The major drawback is the rust which can form if the pan is not thoroughly dried after washing. A cast-iron skillet is ideal for heavy-duty cooking such as preparing the everything-in-one-pan main-dish meals that follow. They're all made in a skillet, using packaged and frozen ingredients, combined with meat, fish or poultry. All you do is toss everything into a skillet (or, at the most, brown the meat first) then cook a bit. Serve with a salad and you have a complete, hassle-free meal!

HAM AND POTATOES AU GRATIN

No need to pare potatoes or make a sauce for this creamy, convenient dish.

Makes 6 servings.

- **1 ham steak, cut about ½-inch thick (about 1¾ pounds)**
- **1 medium-size onion, sliced**
- **1 package (5.5 ounces) au gratin potatoes**
- **2¼ cups boiling water**
- **⅔ cup milk**

1. Trim fat from ham; heat fat in skillet to render about 2 tablespoons of fat drippings. Remove fat pieces; discard. Sauté onion in drippings until soft.

2. Stir in potato slices, sauce mix, boiling water and the milk. Cut ham into bite-size pieces; add to potatoes. Bring to boiling, stirring frequently; lower heat; cover. Simmer 30 minutes or until potatoes are tender and ham is piping hot. Garnish with parsley, if you wish.

ITALIAN SAUSAGES WITH VEGETABLES

Makes 4 servings.

- **1 pound sweet or hot Italian sausages, or a combination of both**
- **½ cup chopped celery**
- **1 package (10 ounces) frozen baby lima beans**
- **2 cans (12 ounces each) whole-kernel corn with sweet peppers**

1. Cut sausages into ½-inch slices. Cook in large skillet until well browned, 15 minutes. Push sausages to one side; sauté celery until soft.

2. Stir in frozen limas and corn. Simmer 10 minutes or until heated through.

CHICKEN RISOTTO

Makes 4 servings.

- **1 broiler-fryer (2½ pounds), cut up**
- **1 package (7½ ounces) risotto rice mix**
- **1 can condensed chicken broth**
  Water
- **1 jar (3 ounces) pimiento-stuffed olives, drained**

1. Place chicken pieces, skin-side down, in a large skillet over very low heat. (Do not add fat.) Cook chicken slowly in its own fat until skin side is a rich brown, about 10 minutes; turn; brown other side. Remove chicken from skillet with tongs.

2. Add rice and seasoning packet from mix to pan drippings; stir to coat rice with drippings.

3. Pour chicken broth into a 4-cup measure; add water to measure 2½ cups. Stir into rice mixture; bring to boiling. Arrange chicken pieces over mixture. Lower heat; cover. Simmer 20 minutes or until chicken is tender and liquid is absorbed. Stir in olives; fluff up rice.

PORK CHOPS WITH RED CABBAGE

Makes 4 servings.

- **4 loin pork chops, cut 1-inch thick (1¾ pounds)**
- **1 large onion, chopped (1 cup)**
- **1 jar (15 ounces) sweet/sour red cabbage**
- **1 small red apple, quartered, cored and sliced**

1. Place pork chops in a large skillet over low heat. (Do not add fat.) Cook chops slowly in their own fat until brown; turn; brown other side. Remove.

2. Add onion to fat in skillet; sauté 5 minutes. Arrange pork chops over onions. Lower heat; cover. Cook 30 minutes, turning once. Remove cover; cook, turning chops once or twice until glazed and most of the liquid has evaporated. Remove chops; keep warm.

3. Drain liquid from cabbage; stir cabbage into skillet with apple slices; cook until heated thoroughly. Arrange pork chops over mixture.

Overleaf: (Clockwise from top left) Italian Sausages with Vegetables, page 627; Chicken Risotto, page 627; Ham and Potatoes au Gratin, page 627; Pork Chops with Red Cabbage, page 627

Skillet Cookery

VEAL SCALLOPS IN MUSHROOM SAUCE

A quick and tasty dish that uses soup as a sauce.

Makes 4 servings.

- 1 **pound veal for scaloppine**
  OR: **1 pound boneless chicken breasts**
- 2 **tablespoons vegetable oil**
- 1 **can (7½ ounces) semi-condensed cream of mushroom soup with wine**
- ½ **teaspoon leaf thyme, crumbled**

1. Pound veal or chicken between two pieces of wax paper until very thin; pat dry on paper toweling. Heat oil in large skillet; sauté veal quickly until it turns white.

2. Stir in soup and thyme; lower heat; simmer just until heated through, about 10 minutes. Taste; add salt and pepper, if you wish. Serve with buttered spinach noodles, if you wish.

BRAISED LAMB CHOPS WITH VEGETABLES

A quick, delicious version of lamb stew.

Makes 4 servings.

- 4 **shoulder lamb chops, cut ½-inch thick (about 1¾ pounds)**
- 1 **can condensed cream of celery soup**
- 1 **package (1 pound, 8 ounces) frozen stew vegetables**
- ½ **teaspoon leaf rosemary, crumbled**

1. Place lamb chops in a large skillet over low heat. (Do not add fat.) Cook chops slowly in their own melting fat until brown; turn and brown other side; remove.

2. Add soup to skillet, scraping up browned bits on bottom of pan. Stir in stew vegetables and rosemary. (Do not add water.)

3. Arrange lamb chops over vegetables. Cover. Simmer, stirring occa-

sionally, 30 minutes or until lamb chops are tender.

BEEF STROGANOFF

Serve this favorite over buttered noodles.

Makes 6 servings.

- 1½ **pounds boneless round steak**
- ½ **envelope (2 tablespoons) onion soup mix**
- 1 **can (6 ounces) sliced mushrooms**
- 1 **container (8 ounces) dairy sour cream**

1. Trim fat from meat; cut fat into cubes; brown cubes in large skillet until fat is rendered. Remove fat pieces with slotted spoon; discard.

2. Cut meat into ¼-inch strips, 2 to 3 inches long, for quick cooking. Add a quarter of the meat to skillet; brown quickly. Remove with slotted spoon to bowl. Repeat until all meat is cooked, then return meat to skillet.

3. Stir in onion soup mix and mushrooms with liquid; heat until bubbly. Slowly stir in sour cream until thoroughly blended. Cook, stirring constantly, until heated thoroughly. Serve over buttered noodles, if you wish.

CHICKEN CACCIATORE

No one will guess you haven't worked on this all day.

Makes 4 servings.

- 1 **broiler-fryer (2½ pounds), cut up**
- 1 **medium-size onion, chopped (½ cup)**
- 1 **jar (14 ounces) spaghetti sauce with peppers and mushrooms**
- 1½ **teaspoons chopped fresh basil**
  OR: ½ **teaspoon dried basil, crumbled**

1. Dry chicken well; place pieces, skin-side down, in large skillet over very low heat. (Do not add fat.) Cook chicken slowly in its own fat until skin side is a rich brown, about 10 minutes; turn; brown other side.

2. Push chicken to one side; sauté onion in drippings until soft. Stir in spaghetti sauce and basil; cover and

simmer 20 minutes. Taste; add salt, if you wish. Serve with spaghetti and crusty bread, if you wish.

CHICKEN LIVERS WITH BACON AND GREEN BEANS

A tasty way to use economical and nutritious chicken livers.

Makes 4 servings.

- 1 **pound chicken livers**
- 4 **bacon slices**
- 2 **tablespoons flour**
- ¼ **cup water**
- 1 **package (9 ounces) frozen Italian green beans**

1. Trim livers of any connective tissue or fat. Cook bacon in large skillet; remove to paper toweling; crumble and reserve. Pour bacon drippings into a cup; measure and return 2 tablespoons to skillet.

2. Roll chicken livers in flour to coat. Brown on all sides in drippings (5 to 10 minutes). Stir in water, scraping up brown bits from skillet. Add beans; cover and cook 10 minutes until beans are tender. Livers should be brown outside and slightly pink inside. Taste; add salt and pepper, if you wish. Sprinkle with crumbled bacon. Serve with fried rice, if you wish.

———— •●• ————

SMELT Small, smooth, shiny silver fish that live in the sea and migrate to rivers and lakes to spawn. The word smelt is derived from "smoelt," an Anglo-Saxon word meaning smooth or shining. Smelts are widely distributed in the western Atlantic, the Pacific Ocean, Arctic Sea and the Great Lakes. Smelts are a popular fish in Europe where they are found from the eastern Atlantic to the Baltic Sea.

Smelts average about 5 to 8 inches in length. Their flesh is rich and oily. Usually the soft bones are eaten along with the fish.

Buying and Storing: Fresh smelts are marketed whole or gutted. Frozen smelts are pan-dressed. Store fresh smelts in the coldest part of the refrigerator. Use within a few days or wrap in moisture-proof paper and freeze for longer storage.

To Prepare and Cook: Rinse smelts with water; pat dry with paper toweling. They can be cooked in a number of ways but frying is the most popular. Coat smelts with flour; dip into beaten egg and recoat with flour or seasoned bread crumbs. Fry in a skillet with a bit of hot oil and butter until golden brown. Smelts can also be dipped in a thin batter and deep-fat fried. Drain and serve with lemon wedges.

SMOKED MEAT Foods such as ham, pork, bacon and sausages that are flavored and preserved by smoking. The meat is first cured or salted, then it is hung or placed in a chamber where a wood-chip fire is smoldering into a dense smoke. The smoke flavors the food and the heat dries the food to aid in preserving it. The flavor of the smoke will depend on the type of wood burned. Oak and hickory are the most popular but juniper and beech are also used. Smoking was one of the most convenient and reliable methods of preserving meat for long storage before the invention of refrigerators and freezers. See also **HAM, BACON.**

SNOW PEA See **PEA.**

SOLE Although a number of flat fish in the market bear the name "sole," such as "gray sole," "lemon sole," or "white sole," they are not true soles. Gray or white sole is actually witch flounder; lemon sole is winter flounder. The true soles in the western Atlantic are too small to be commercially marketed. The Dover sole, available frozen or air-freighted fresh from Europe, is the only true sole obtainable. The Dover sole is found from the Mediterranean to Denmark. It is about 12 inches long, oval and flat in shape. Its flesh is lean, firm and fine textured.

The other fish which are marketed as "sole" belong to other families of flat fish. Their body shape is round rather than elliptical. They are sold whole or in fillets, fresh or frozen. They are a lean, delicately flavored fish. They can be poached and sauced, sautéed, broiled or baked.

SOLE BONNE FEMME

Bonne Femme means "good wife" and in this recipe means fish, the way a good wife cooks it.

Bake at 450° for 10 minutes.
Makes 4 servings.

- 1 **pound fresh or thawed, frozen fillets of sole**
- 1 **can (3 or 4 ounces) sliced mushrooms**
- 2 **tablespoons instant minced onion**
- ½ **cup dry sherry**
- ½ **teaspoon salt**
   Pinch of white pepper
- 1 **tablespoon dried parsley flakes**
- ½ **cup milk**
- 1 **tablespoon flour**
   Paprika

1. Thaw the fillets. Pour mushrooms with their liquid into a shallow, 6-cup, flameproof dish. Sprinkle with the onion. Place the fillets over the mushrooms, folding to fit. Pour the sherry over fish; sprinkle with salt, pepper and parsley flakes.
2. Bake in very hot oven (450°) for 10 minutes.
3. Carefully drain the liquid from the fish into a small saucepan. Cook quickly over high heat until liquid is reduced by half. Combine milk with flour; stir into liquid. Cook, stirring constantly, until the sauce thickens and bubbles. Pour over fish; sprinkle with paprika. Broil 4 inches from heat, about 3 minutes or until top is lightly browned and bubbly.

SOLE-ALMOND BAKE

Bake at 375° for 15 minutes.
Makes 6 servings.

- 2 **packages (1 pound each) frozen fillets of sole**
- ½ **cup all-purpose flour**
- 2 **teaspoons salt**
- 1 **teaspoon paprika**
- ½ **teaspoon leaf thyme, crumbled**
- ¼ **teaspoon pepper**
- 2 **eggs**
- 2 **tablespoons dry white wine or milk**

- ¾ **cup chopped blanched almonds**
- 2 **tablespoons melted butter or margarine**

1. Defrost fish following label directions. Pat dry on paper toweling.
2. Combine flour, salt, paprika, thyme and pepper on wax paper.
3. In shallow dish, stir together eggs and wine.
4. Coat fish with flour then dip into egg mixture; roll in almonds.
5. Place fish in well-greased baking pan. Drizzle melted butter over.
6. Bake in a moderate oven (375°) for 15 minutes or until fish flakes easily. Thicker pieces will take longer.

GOURMET SOLE VÉRONIQUE

Simply elegant—sole in a silky, grape-garnished sauce.

Bake at 350° for 25 minutes.
Makes 4 servings.

- 1 **can condensed chicken broth**
- 1 **soup can water**
- ⅛ **teaspoon salt**
   Dash white pepper
- ⅛ **teaspoon bouquet garni for fish**
- 12 **seedless green grapes, halved**
- 1 **package (1 pound) frozen fillets of sole, thawed**
- ¼ **cup (½ stick) butter or margarine**
- ¼ **cup all-purpose flour**
- 2 **tablespoons dry white wine**

1. Combine chicken broth, water, salt, pepper, bouquet garni and grapes in a large skillet; bring to boiling.
2. Separate the fillets; place in pan; cover. Simmer 5 to 8 minutes.
3. Lift the fillets from liquid with a pancake turner; place in a shallow baking dish. Pour liquid into a 2-cup measure; add water, if necessary, to make 2 cups.
4. Melt butter in a medium-size saucepan; stir in the flour. Cook slowly, stirring constantly, until bubbly. Stir in the 2 cups liquid; continue cooking and stirring until the sauce thickens and bubbles for 3 minutes. Stir in wine; pour over fish.
5. Bake in moderate oven (350°) for 25 minutes or until fish flakes easily.

●●●

Sorrel

SORREL Also known as dock, sorrel is a sour-tasting, leafy green plant that is eaten as a cooked vegetable, made into soups or sauces, or added raw to salads. There are several varieties cultivated which differ in leaf shape and flavor. The most common is called garden sorrel. The leaves are a light, dull green, narrow and arrowhead-shaped. Its high oxalic acid content gives the leaves a sour flavor. French sorrel is another variety. It has shield-shaped leaves which are not as sour as garden sorrel. The mildest variety is called spinach dock. It has very long green leaves. Wild sorrel, found in many fields, is called oxalis, wood sorrel, sour grass or sour clover. The leaves are small and light green.

SOUFFLÉ A light, puffy egg dish that is sweet or savory. The classic soufflé is baked and should rise above its dish. It must be served immediately. It can be flavored with cheese, vegetables, seafood, vanilla or chocolate. Nowadays, a cold soufflé is made with gelatin added. In order to have the appearance of having risen, a collar is wrapped around the dish. After the dish is filled and chilled, the collar is removed.

FRESH APPLE NOUGAT SOUFFLÉ

Makes 8 servings.

    3 to 4 medium-size apples
    ½ cup apple juice or water
    1 envelope unflavored gelatin
    ½ cup sugar
    ½ teaspoon ground cinnamon
    ⅛ teaspoon ground nutmeg
    5 eggs, separated
    ½ cup heavy cream, whipped
    1 cup crushed Walnut Nougat
      (recipe follows)

1. Prepare a 5-cup soufflé or other straight-sided glass dish with a collar this way: Fold a 24-inch length of wax paper in half lengthwise; wrap around dish to make a 2-inch collar. Fasten with tape or string.
2. Pare, quarter, core and slice apples (You'll have about 4 cups.) Sprinkle with ¼ cup of the apple juice. Cook, covered, over low heat, just until apples are tender, about 10 minutes.
3. While apples are cooking, sprinkle gelatin over remaining apple juice in a medium-size bowl. Let stand 5 minutes to soften.
4. Beat ¼ cup of the sugar, the cinnamon, nutmeg and egg yolks into softened gelatin. Beat mixture well; add to apples all at once, beating constantly. Remove from heat; pour into medium-size bowl. Chill, stirring often, just until mixture mounds slightly when spooned.
5. Beat egg whites in a large bowl until foamy-white. Gradually beat in remaining ¼ cup sugar until meringue stands in soft peaks. Fold meringue, then whipped cream, into chilled apple mixture until no streaks of white remain. Fold in nougat. Pour into prepared dish. Refrigerate until firm, about 4 hours.
6. To serve: Gently remove collar. Garnish with additional whipped cream and apple slices, if you wish. Sprinkle edge with crushed Walnut Nougat.

Walnut Nougat: Combine 5 tablespoons butter, ½ cup sugar, 1 tablespoon honey and 1 tablespoon water in small heavy saucepan. Cook, stirring often, over medium-high heat until candy thermometer reaches 300° to 305°, about 5 minutes. Add ½ cup coarsely chopped walnuts; mix well. Pour onto buttered cookie sheet. Cool completely. When candy is cooled and hardened, chop or crush into small pieces. Makes about 1½ cups crushed.

Note: Keep any extra Walnut Nougat in tightly covered jar to sprinkle on ice cream or breakfast cereal.

HOT CHOCOLATE SOUFFLÉ

Bake at 350° for 50 minutes.
Makes 6 servings.

    ½ cup sugar
    3 tablespoons flour
    ¼ teaspoon salt
    1 cup milk
    3 squares unsweetened
      chocolate
    2 tablespoons butter or
      margarine
    1 teaspoon vanilla
    4 egg yolks
    6 egg whites, at room
      temperature
      Sugar

1. Coat a 6-cup soufflé dish well with soft butter or margarine; sprinkle evenly with sugar, tapping out excess. Fold a 24-inch piece of foil in thirds lengthwise; butter on one side; wrap around dish, buttered-side in, to make a 2-inch collar. Tie with string. Sprinkle paper with sugar.
2. Blend 6 tablespoons of the sugar with the flour and salt in small saucepan. Gradually stir in milk; add chocolate. Cook over medium heat, stirring constantly, until the chocolate is melted and mixture thickens and bubbles 2 minutes. Remove from heat; stir in butter and vanilla. Preheat oven to 350°.
3. Beat egg yolks in small bowl with wire whisk; add slightly cooled chocolate mixture.
4. Beat egg whites in large bowl until soft peaks form when beater is raised. Add remaining 2 tablespoons sugar, 1 tablespoon at a time, beating until shiny and stiff peaks form when beaters are raised.
5. Stir about ¼ of egg white mixture into chocolate mixture, then add to remaining whites and gently fold in. Pour mixture into prepared dish; sprinkle top lightly with sugar. Place dish in baking pan on oven rack; pour boiling water into pan to depth of 1 inch.
6. Bake in a preheated moderate oven (350°) for 50 minutes or until light and puffy. To serve: Remove collar; serve immediately with ice cold whipped cream, a custard sauce or warm chocolate sauce, if you wish.

TWIN ZABAGLIONE SOUFFLÉS

Makes 8 servings.

    1 envelope unflavored gelatin
    ¼ cup water
    7 egg yolks
    ¾ cup sugar
    ⅔ cup Marsala or sherry
    1 tablespoon instant espresso
      powder
    4 egg whites

½ cup heavy cream, whipped
Whipped cream
Chocolate curls

1. Prepare a 5-cup soufflé dish or straight-sided glass dish with a collar this way: Fold a 24-inch length of 12-inch-wide foil in thirds lengthwise; wrap around dish to make a 2-inch collar. Fasten with tape or string. To make divider for the two mixtures: Tear off a length of foil that will just fit vertically inside the dish. Fold in thirds and stand it inside dish. Tape to collar at top.

2. Sprinkle gelatin over water in a 1-cup measure. Let stand 5 minutes to soften. Set cup in a saucepan of simmering water, stirring until gelatin is completely dissolved.

3. Beat egg yolks and ½ cup of the sugar slightly in top of double boiler. Beat in all but 1 tablespoon of the Marsala. Place over simmering, not boiling, water.

4. Cook, beating constantly with rotary hand mixer or portable electric mixer at medium speed, until mixture thickens slightly and is more than double in volume. This will take about 20 minutes. Remove double boiler top from water; add gelatin and continue beating a few minutes longer. Divide mixture evenly between 2 medium-size bowls.

5. Dissolve espresso in reserved tablespoon of Marsala; beat into mixture in one of the bowls. Chill both bowls until mixture mounds slightly when spooned.

6. Beat egg whites until foamy; gradually beat in remaining sugar and continue beating until meringue stands in soft peaks.

7. Fold half the meringue and half the whipped cream into each bowl of gelatin mixture. Spoon both mixtures simultaneously into prepared dish, placing espresso mixture on one side of the divider and plain mixture on the other. When dish is full, gently pull divider out, scraping off each side. Refrigerate 4 hours.

8. To serve: Remove collar carefully; garnish with additional whipped cream and curls or gratings of semi-sweet chocolate.

CORN AND CHEESE SOUFFLÉ

Bake at 350° for 50 minutes.
Makes 6 servings.

  6 eggs
  2 tablespoons packaged bread crumbs
  2 cups whole-kernel corn (from 4 ears)
  6 tablespoons butter
  ¼ teaspoon pepper
  ⅓ cup chopped green onions
  ⅓ cup all-purpose flour
  1 teaspoon salt
  ½ teaspoon dry mustard
1¾ cups milk
  3 ounces Swiss cheese, shredded (¾ cup)
     Few drops liquid hot pepper seasoning

1. Separate eggs, placing yolks in large bowl and whites in medium-size bowl. Reserve.

2. Butter a 2-quart soufflé dish; sprinkle bottom and side with bread crumbs.

3. Sauté corn in 1 tablespoon of the butter in skillet for 5 minutes. Remove from heat. Sprinkle with pepper.

4. Sauté onions in remaining 5 tablespoons butter in medium-size saucepan; stir in flour, salt and mustard; cook and stir until mixture bubbles 1 minute. Gradually stir in 1½ cups of the milk. Cook and stir until mixture thickens and bubbles 3 minutes. Remove from heat. Preheat oven to 350°.

5. Stir ⅓ cup of the sauce and the remaining ¼ cup milk into the corn. Spoon corn mixture into bottom of prepared dish.

6. Stir cheese and liquid hot pepper into remaining sauce in pan. Beat egg yolks slightly with fork. Gradually beat in the sauce until thoroughly blended.

7. Beat egg whites until they form soft peaks. Stir ¼ of the whites into the sauce until well mixed. Gently fold remaining whites into sauce until no streaks of white remain. Do not over-mix. Spoon over corn in dish.

8. Bake in a preheated moderate oven (350°) for 50 minutes or until puffy and golden brown.

INDIVIDUAL ORANGE SOUFFLÉS

Fragrant and fragile, yet easy to make, these tiny orange dessert soufflés are a pure pleasure to eat.

Bake at 375° for 18 minutes.
Makes 6 servings.

  ¼ cup (½ stick) sweet butter
  ½ cup all-purpose flour
  ⅓ cup plus 1½ tablespoons sugar
1½ cups milk, scalded
  2 large navel oranges
  5 egg yolks
  2 tablespoons Grand Marnier
  6 egg whites
     10X (confectioners') sugar

1. Butter 8 small individual soufflé dishes or 6 slightly larger ones. Dust lightly with sugar; shake out the excess.

2. Melt the butter in a saucepan. Blend in the flour; cook, stirring constantly, 1 to 2 minutes. Cool slightly.

3. Add the sugar to milk; stir to dissolve. Whisk milk mixture rapidly into the *roux* until smooth. Cook, stirring constantly, until mixture thickens and comes to a boil. Remove from heat.

4. Grate rind from oranges; then peel and section. Preheat oven to 375°.

5. Whisk egg yolks, grated orange rind and Grand Marnier into hot mixture. Beat egg whites until stiff but not dry; fold into hot mixture.

6. Fill prepared soufflé dishes ⅓ full with soufflé mixture. Divide the orange sections among the dishes. Add enough soufflé mixture to ¾ fill each dish. Smooth surfaces.

7. Bake in a preheated moderate oven (375°) for 18 minutes or until soufflés are puffed and golden brown. Sprinkle tops with 10X sugar and *serve at once,* while puffed and perfect. Any extra soufflé mixture can be warmed in a double boiler over hot, not boiling, water, thinned down with orange juice; serve as a sauce. *Note:* The same mixture can, of course, be baked in a single large soufflé dish (filled ¾ full). Bake at 325° for 20 minutes, increase oven temperature to 350° and bake 10 minutes longer or until soufflé is well-puffed and golden brown. ●●●

SOUP The word comes from the Latin *suppa*. It is basically a liquid food that can be served as a main course or appetizer. A soup can be clear or creamy, hearty or light, sweet or savory, hot or cold.

Making soup from scratch is an old-fashioned way of cutting food costs which still holds true today. A soup kettle can be the repository for odds and ends of vegetables and meat or poultry bones. If time is short, rely on canned broths and soup mixes. For more recipes, see **BROTH**.

SOUP ITALIANO

Makes 6 servings.

- 4 slices hard salami, cut into julienne strips
- 2 teaspoons butter or margarine
- 1 cup shredded cabbage
- 1 can (19 ounces) chunky vegetable soup
- 1 can (20 ounces) chick-peas, drained
- 1 can (16 ounces) round bite-size ravioli in meat sauce
- 1 can condensed beef broth
- 1¼ cups water
- 1 teaspoon Italian herb seasoning mix
  Grated Parmesan cheese

1. Brown salami in butter in a large saucepan. Stir in cabbage; cook 1 minute. Add soup, chick-peas, ravioli, broth, water and Italian seasoning. Heat slowly to boiling; lower heat; simmer 2 minutes.
2. Ladle into large heated soup bowls and sprinkle with Parmesan cheese. Top with croutons, if you wish.

CHICKEN RICE SOUP

Makes 12 one-cup servings.

- 1 broiler-fryer (2 pounds)
- 4½ cups water
- 1 onion, quartered
- 1 bay leaf
- 6 sprigs parsley
  Celery tops
- 2 cans (16 ounces each) tomatoes
- 1 potato, diced (1 cup)
- 1 large onion, diced (1 cup)
- 1 green pepper, seeded and diced (1 cup)
- 2 carrots, diced (1 cup)
- ½ cup uncooked long-grain rice
- 1 tablespoon salt
- ½ teaspoon pepper
- 2 envelopes instant chicken broth

1. Place chicken and water in Dutch oven. Add onion, bay leaf, parsley and celery tops. Bring to boiling. Lower heat; cover and cook 1 hour or until chicken is tender. Remove solids from broth to bowl; strain broth; return broth to Dutch oven.
2. While chicken is cooling, prepare vegetables. Add tomatoes, potato, onion, green pepper, carrots, rice, salt, pepper and instant chicken broth to broth in Dutch oven. Simmer, covered, 30 minutes.
3. When chicken is cool enough to handle, skin and bone and cut meat into small pieces (about 2½ cups). Add to soup. Cover and cook 15 minutes or until vegetables and rice are tender.

GARDEN VEGETABLE SOUP

Makes 8 cups.

- 2 tablespoons butter or margarine
- 2 tablespoons vegetable oil
- 1 cup sliced carrots
- 1 cup sliced celery, with some of the green leafy tops
- 1 large onion, chopped (1 cup)
- 1 clove garlic, crushed
- 9 medium-size tomatoes
  OR: 2 cans (16 ounces each) tomatoes, undrained
- 1 teaspoon leaf oregano, crumbled
- 1 teaspoon leaf basil, crumbled
- 2 teaspoons salt
- ¼ teaspoon pepper
- 1 can (13¾ ounces) beef broth
- ¼ pound green beans, washed, trimmed and cut into 1-inch pieces (1 cup)
- ½ pound zucchini, cut in half lengthwise and thinly sliced (2 cups)
- ¼ cup chopped fresh parsley
  Grated Parmesan cheese

1. Heat butter and oil in Dutch oven; sauté carrots, celery, onion and garlic, 5 minutes.
2. Peel tomatoes; cut in half crosswise. Place strainer over large bowl; remove seeds by squeezing gently. Chop pulp and add to juice in large bowl.
3. Add tomatoes and juice to Dutch oven; add oregano, basil, salt and pepper; cook 15 minutes.
4. Add beef broth and green beans; cook 30 minutes longer, adding zucchini and parsley after 20 minutes. Serve with Parmesan cheese.

ITALIAN MEATBALL AND ESCAROLE SOUP

Serve this one-pot supper soup with crusty whole-wheat Italian bread and a salad of crunchy raw vegetables.

Makes 6 servings.

- 1 pound ground beef
- 1 egg
- 3 tablespoons water
- 3 cloves garlic, minced
- 2 tablespoons chopped fresh parsley
- 1 teaspoon salt
- ¼ teaspoon pepper
- ½ cup uncooked long-grain rice
- 2 tablespoons butter
- 8 cups homemade or canned chicken broth
- ¾ pound escarole, rinsed and chopped (about 12 cups)
- 2 tablespoons lemon juice
  Freshly grated Parmesan cheese

1. Combine the beef with the egg, water, 2 cloves garlic, parsley, salt and pepper in a medium-size bowl and blend thoroughly. Shape mixture into 32 small meatballs.
2. Sauté rice and remaining clove garlic in the butter in a large skillet, about 5 minutes or until golden.
3. Bring the broth to boiling in a kettle or Dutch oven.
4. Add meatballs and rice to boiling broth; lower heat; cover; simmer 15 minutes or until meatballs are cooked throughout. (Test one to check.)
5. Add escarole and lemon juice, recover and cook 5 minutes longer. Serve Parmesan cheese separately.

Soup

CHILLED BLUEBERRY SOUP

Makes 6 servings.

- 1 **thin strip lemon rind (yellow part only)**
- 1 **3-inch piece stick cinnamon**
- 3 **whole cloves**
- 1 **pint fresh blueberries**
- 3 **cups water**
- 6 to 8 **tablespoons sugar**
- ½ **cup port wine**
- ¼ **cup orange juice**
- 1 **container (8 ounces) dairy sour cream**

1. Tie lemon rind, cinnamon and cloves in a small piece of cheesecloth. Combine with blueberries, water and sugar in a medium-size saucepan.
2. Bring to boiling; lower heat; cover. Simmer 10 minutes or until berries begin to burst and turn soft. Remove spice bag. Cool slightly.
3. Pour soup, part at a time, into container of electric blender; cover. Whirl until smooth.
4. Pour through sieve into a large bowl. Stir in port wine and orange juice. Cover; chill several hours, preferably overnight.
5. Pour into chilled serving bowl. Garnish with dollops of sour cream. Serve icy cold.

CREAM OF FRESH TOMATO SOUP

Makes 6 servings.

- 3 **medium-size very ripe tomatoes**
- 1 **small onion, finely chopped (¼ cup)**
- ½ **cup finely chopped celery**
  Pinch sugar (optional)
- 3 **whole cloves**
- 1 **small bay leaf**
- 3 **tablespoons butter**
- 3 **tablespoons flour**
- 1 **teaspoon salt**
- 3 **cups milk**

1. Peel and chop tomatoes; combine with onion, celery, sugar (if used), cloves and bay leaf in a medium-size saucepan. Bring to boiling; lower heat; cover and simmer 15 minutes.
2. Melt butter in a large saucepan. Stir in flour and salt; cook 1 minute; stir in milk. Cook, stirring constantly, until mixture thickens and bubbles, 2

minutes; keep warm.
3. Puree tomato mixture through sieve or food mill. Stir puree slowly into sauce. Heat but do not boil. Serve with croutons, if you wish.

FRESH GREEN PEA SOUP

Makes 8 servings.

- 4 **cups shelled fresh peas (4 pounds)**
  OR: 2 **packages (10 ounces each) frozen peas**
- ½ **cup coarsely chopped leeks**
- ½ **cup water or chicken broth**
- 2 **sprigs mint**
  OR: ½ **teaspoon dried mint**
- 1 **teaspoon salt**
- ½ **teaspoon leaf chervil, crumbled**
- ½ **teaspoon leaf basil, crumbled**
- ¼ **teaspoon leaf marjoram, crumbled**
- ¼ **teaspoon leaf thyme, crumbled**
- ¼ **teaspoon white pepper**
- 1 **tablespoon sugar** (optional)
- 1½ **quarts milk, at room temperature**

1. Combine peas, leeks and water in a medium-size saucepan; bring just to boiling, but do not boil.
2. Whirl peas and liquid, mint leaves, salt, chervil, basil, marjoram, thyme, white pepper, sugar and just enough of the milk to liquefy peas in container of electric blender until smooth.
3. Pour mixture into saucepan; add remaining milk. Heat through. Garnish with mint sprigs, if you wish.

--- ●●● ---

SOUR CREAM Sometimes called dairy or cultured sour cream, it is made from cream to which a lactic acid culture has been added and allowed to ripen or sour. The cream used has been pasteurized (heated to 145°F. to destroy any harmful bacteria) and homogenized (to distribute the fat evenly). Commercially-made sour cream has a fat content of 18 to 20 percent, similar to light cream. A tablespoon of sour cream contains 25 calories.

Sour cream can curdle if cooked over too high a temperature. In most recipes, sour cream is stirred in near the end of the cooking time and never allowed to come to a boil.

SOUR CREAM POUND CAKE

This fine-textured cake has a lovely flavor and keeps well.

Bake at 325° for 1 hour and 30 minutes.

Makes 1 ten-inch tube cake.

- 1 **cup (2 sticks) butter, softened**
- 3 **cups sugar**
- 6 **eggs, separated**
- 1 **teaspoon lemon extract**
- 1 **teaspoon vanilla**
- ¼ **teaspoon baking soda**
- 1 **container (8 ounces) dairy sour cream**
- 3⅓ **cups** *sifted* **all-purpose flour**

1. Grease and flour a 10×4-inch angel-cake tube pan. Preheat oven to 325°.
2. Beat butter and 2½ cups of the sugar in a large bowl with electric mixer until well blended. Add egg yolks, 1 at a time, and continue beating until mixture is creamy-light; add lemon extract and vanilla.
3. Beat egg whites in a medium-size bowl until foamy-white. Add remaining ½ cup sugar, 1 tablespoon at a time, beating until mixture forms soft, glossy peaks.
4. Stir baking soda into sour cream. Add flour alternately with sour cream mixture to butter mixture, blending well after each addition. Fold in beaten egg white mixture until no streaks of white remain. Pour into prepared pan.
5. Bake in a preheated slow oven (325°) for 1 hour and 30 minutes or until cake tester or wooden pick inserted near center comes out clean. Cool in pan on wire rack 10 minutes. Loosen around edge and tube; remove from pan; cool completely.

GARLIC CHEESE DIP

Makes 2 cups.

- 1 **container (16 ounces) dairy sour cream**
- 1 **envelope cheese-garlic salad dressing mix**
- ½ **teaspoon dried parsley flakes**

Combine sour cream, salad dressing mix and parsley flakes in a small bowl; chill for several hours to blend flavors.

Pictured opposite: Garden Vegetable Soup, page 635

Sour Cream

GREEN BEANS WITH SOUR CREAM

This is a terrific way to cook beans. Prepare the vegetables and put them in the casserole before you make the sauce.

Bake at 400° for 15 to 20 minutes.
Makes 6 to 8 servings.

- **1 medium-size onion, minced (½ cup)**
- **2 packages (9 ounces each) frozen French-cut green beans, cooked**
- **1 teaspoon sugar**
- **2 tablespoons butter or margarine**
- **1 tablespoon flour**
- **1 teaspoon salt**
- **½ teaspoon pepper**
- **1 container (8 ounces) dairy sour cream**
- **2 tablespoons shredded Swiss cheese**
- **2 tablespoons chopped almonds**

1. Mix onion, beans and sugar in a buttered 1½-quart casserole.
2. Melt butter in a saucepan until foamy; stir in flour. Cook 1 minute. Add salt, pepper and sour cream; heat, but do not boil. Spoon sauce over vegetables and toss lightly until thoroughly mixed. Sprinkle with cheese and almonds.
3. Bake in a hot oven (400°) for 15 to 20 minutes.

ONION AND BACON BREAD

Bake at 425° for 25 minutes.
Makes one 8-inch round loaf.

- **3 bacon slices**
- **2 large onions, sliced (2 cups)**
- **2 tablespoons chopped fresh parsley**
- **2 cups buttermilk baking mix**
- **½ cup milk**
- **1 container (8 ounces) dairy sour cream**
- **1 egg, slightly beaten**
- **½ teaspoon salt**

1. Cook bacon until crisp in large skillet; remove bacon; drain on paper toweling; crumble and reserve.
2. Sauté onions in bacon drippings just until soft but not brown. Remove from heat; stir in parsley.
3. Mix baking mix and milk in a medium-size bowl; stir with fork just until blended. Spread in lightly greased 8×1½-inch layer-cake pan. Spoon onion mixture on top. Preheat oven to 425°.
4. Blend sour cream, egg and salt in small bowl. Spoon over onion layer. Sprinkle with reserved bacon; mix partially into cream with fork.
5. Bake in a preheated hot oven (425°) for 25 minutes or until the topping is set and begins to brown. Cool on a wire rack. Cut into wedges and serve warm.

SOUR CREAM CAKE WITH COCONUT TOPPING

So quick to whip up when you're expecting a neighbor to stop by.

Bake at 350° for 35 minutes.
Makes one 8-inch square cake.

- **1 container (8 ounces) dairy sour cream**
- **2 eggs**
- **¾ cup sugar**
- **1½ cups *sifted* all-purpose flour**
- **2 teaspoons baking powder**
- **½ to 1 teaspoon almond extract Coconut Topping (recipe follows)**

1. Let sour cream and eggs warm to room temperature for easy mixing. Remove 2 tablespoons sour cream to small bowl; reserve for Coconut Topping. Grease and flour an 8×8×2-inch baking pan. Preheat oven to 350°.
2. Combine remaining sour cream, eggs, sugar, flour, baking powder and almond extract in a large bowl. Beat at medium speed with electric mixer for 1 minute, scraping down side of bowl with plastic spatula. Pour into prepared pan.
3. Bake in a preheated moderate oven (350°) for 25 minutes or until the center springs back when lightly pressed with fingertip.
4. Remove baked cake from oven. Spread Coconut Topping evenly over top. Return to oven. Bake 10 minutes longer. Cool in pan on wire rack.

Coconut Topping: Combine reserved sour cream, 2 tablespoons soft butter, ½ cup firmly packed brown sugar and ½ cup flaked coconut until well mixed.

SOUR CREAM AND HORSERADISH BURGERS

Makes 4 servings.

- **½ cup dairy sour cream**
- **3 tablespoons prepared horseradish**
- **½ teaspoon salt**
- **¼ teaspoon pepper**
- **1 pound ground chuck or round**

1. Combine sour cream, horseradish, salt and pepper in a medium-size bowl; blend well. Add ground chuck and mix lightly with a fork. Shape into 4 equal-size patties. Place on rack over broiler pan.
2. Broil 3 inches from heat about 4 minutes on each side, turning once.

DANISH BEET AND SOUR CREAM SOUP

Makes 8 servings.

- **6 medium-size beets (1½ pounds)**
- **¼ cup (½ stick) butter or margarine**
- **¼ cup all-purpose flour**
- **3 cans (13¾ ounces each) chicken broth**
- **1 container (8 ounces) dairy sour cream**
- **2 tablespoons lemon juice**
- **½ teaspoon salt**
- **⅛ teaspoon freshly ground pepper**
- **2 tablespoons snipped fresh dill or chives**

1. Scrub beets; trim, leaving 1 inch of the tops and the root ends attached. Cook, covered, in boiling salted water to cover, 45 minutes or until tender when pierced with the tip of a sharp knife. Drain; rinse in cold running water; slip off skins, root and top.
2. Chop the beets, reserving ½ cup. Place remaining beets in container of electric blender; reserve.
3. Melt butter in a large saucepan; stir in flour and cook, stirring constantly, for 2 to 3 minutes, without browning. Stir in the broth until smooth. Bring to boiling; lower heat; simmer 5 minutes. Cool, then add a

few spoonfuls to blender with the beets. Whirl until smooth, then pour back into remaining mixture in saucepan. Stir in sour cream, lemon juice, salt and pepper.

4. Heat soup, stirring constantly, but do not boil. If too thick, thin with a little chicken broth. Add the reserved beets and garnish soup with dill or chives.

— ● ● ● —

SOURDOUGH A lump of dough soured or fermented by yeast occurring naturally in the air. It is the basis of sourdough bread, biscuits and flapjacks. Since the days of the Gold Rush, people have been making sourdough bread. The bread is leavened with some of the soured dough which is called "starter." Once the starter is made, you simply measure the amount required for the recipe and replace it with an equal mixture of flour and milk. In the past, only sourdough starter was used to raise the bread—it took 24 hours. To quicken the process, you can add commercial yeast and still get that special sourdough flavor.

SOYBEANS Fresh soybeans sold in their fuzzy green pods are becoming more readily available in the markets. The pods look like pea pods but are much flatter. The shucked pods each contain 3 or 4 beans. The beans can be cooked like peas and served as a vegetable.

Soybean pods grow on bushy plants belonging to the pea family. Believed to be native to southeast Asia, soybeans are an important source of protein in the Far East. Soybeans contain a high-quality vegetable protein, vitamins and minerals but are low in carbohydrates. They have a high fat content. Because soybeans are relatively inexpensive to grow, the low-cost proteins that they provide increase their role in the world's food supply.

In the United States, soybeans are commercially grown for their fat content. The fat is used in making vegetable oil, margarine, soaps and many industrial products. The leftover meal is used as animal feed; some is used for human consumption. It is often made into meat substitutes.

Soybeans have been cultivated in China for over 4,000 years. Soybeans are used to make soy sauce, a salty, brown condiment made from boiled soybeans, roasted wheat flour, salt and yeast which is fermented over a period of time. Bean curd or *tofu* is the fermented milk from the soybean. It is formed into soft or firm cakes and is eaten as a protein food in soups and stir-fried dishes. Soybean sprouts are eaten as a cooked vegetable. Dried soybeans are used for sprouting. Soybean sprouts are the larger bean sprouts that are available in the markets. Mung beans are the smaller bean sprouts which are available fresh or canned.

Dried soybeans are available in specialty food stores. They can be cooked like other dried beans.

Soybean flour, sold in the health-food section of the supermarket, is available with different fat contents. Full-fat soybean flour is made by grinding soybeans that have only the hulls removed. Low-fat flour is made from the meal after all or nearly all the oil is removed from the soybeans. Soy flour is highly flavored and should be mixed with wheat flour in baked goods when gluten is needed.

SOYBEANS AND RICE VEGETABLE BOATS

A puree of soybeans, a handful of chopped parsley and green onions are blended with brown rice for a healthful main dish.

Bake at 375° for 15 minutes.
Makes 4 servings.

- **1 cup dried soybeans**
- **3 cups cold water**
- **1 teaspoon salt**
- **½ cup brown rice, (2 cups) cooked**
- **4 medium-size zucchini**
- **½ cup chopped green onions**
- **½ cup chopped fresh parsley**
- **¼ teaspoon pepper**
- **2 tablespoons butter or margarine**
- **¾ cup plain wheat germ**

1. Pick over soybeans and rinse under running cold water. Cover soybeans with cold water in a glass bowl; cover bowl and let stand overnight at room temperature.

2. Pour soybeans and soaking liquid into a large saucepan; stir in salt. Bring to boiling; cover saucepan; lower heat and simmer 3 hours. (Soybeans will still not be tender.) Drain beans and reserve liquid.

3. While soybeans are cooking, prepare brown rice following label directions.

4. Halve zucchini lengthwise; parboil in boiling salted water in a large skillet 5 minutes; drain, cut-side down, on paper toweling until cool enough to handle. Scoop out seeds with a spoon.

5. Measure ¾ cup soybean liquid into an electric blender container; add cooked soybeans; cover; whirl until mixture is very smooth.

6. Combine soybean puree, cooked brown rice, green onions, parsley and pepper in a medium-size bowl.

7. Arrange zucchini, cut-side up, in a shallow 8-cup baking dish; fill zucchini shells with soybean mixture. Melt butter in a small saucepan; stir in wheat germ until well-blended. Sprinkle over zucchini shells.

8. Bake in a moderate oven (375°) for 15 minutes or until topping is golden and shells are heated through.

SOY-FLOUR WAFFLES

Makes 6 waffles.

- **1¾ cups all-purpose flour**
- **¼ cup low-fat soy flour**
- **¼ teaspoon baking soda**
- **1½ teaspoons baking powder**
- **2 eggs, separated**
- **1¾ cups buttermilk**
- **5 tablespoons melted butter or margarine**

1. Sift dry ingredients together into bowl.

2. Beat egg yolks in a separate bowl until light. Add buttermilk and butter to egg yolks; beat; add to dry ingredients, combining with a few strokes.

3. Beat egg whites until stiff; fold into batter. Cook in a nonstick waffle iron.

— ● ● ● —

Soy Sauce

SOY SAUCE An essential ingredient in Oriental cooking, soy sauce is a savory brown liquid made from fermented soybeans, wheat, yeast and salt. Each producer has his own recipe for soy sauce so that there are variations in flavor and saltiness.

American-made brands of soy sauce are produced by a chemical process rather than natural fermentation. It tends to be very salty and slightly bitter in taste. The American-made Japanese brand of soy sauce available in most supermarkets is naturally brewed. It is slightly sweeter than most of the other American brands.

Imported Chinese soy sauce, available in specialty food stores, is naturally brewed. Sometimes two types are sold —light and dark. Light soy sauce has a thin consistency and a saltier flavor than dark soy sauce. It is used in dishes when the natural color of the foods is to be retained. Dark soy sauce is thick or black because of the caramel coloring added. It has a slightly sweet taste and is ideal for slow-simmered dishes. Often, both types of soy sauce are used in one dish to achieve a desired flavor and color.

Because each brand of soy sauce varies in taste and saltiness, so will the flavor of the prepared dish. Experiment until you find the brand that suits your taste.

GRILLED WHOLE FISH

Makes 12 servings.

- 2 whole dressed red snappers, striped bass or haddock (each weighing 3 to 4 pounds)
- ⅓ cup soy sauce
- ⅓ cup dry sherry
- ¼ cup lemon juice
- 2 tablespoons vegetable oil
- 1 tablespoon finely chopped fresh ginger
- 1 tablespoon sugar
- 6 green onions, sliced
  Lemon slices
  Green onions, cut into 1-inch pieces

1. Make several diagonal incisions in both sides of fish. Place in shallow dish.
2. Combine soy sauce, sherry, lemon juice, oil, ginger, sugar and onions; pour over fish. Marinate, turning fish several times, 1 hour at room temperature; insert pieces of lemon and green onion in slits on both sides. Place fish in a greased hinged broiler.
3. Grill fish over hot coals 4 inches from heat 10 to 15 minutes on each side, brushing several times with marinade or until fish flakes when pierced with a fork. (Fish can be broiled, using a greased broiler pan.) Transfer to heated serving platter. Serve with rice, if you wish.

CHINESE FRIED RICE AND CHICKEN

Makes 4 servings.

- ¼ cup vegetable oil
- 2 eggs, lightly beaten
- 1 cup thinly sliced green onions, including green tops
- 1 cup drained bamboo shoots, sliced
- 3 cups cold cooked rice
- ¼ cup soy sauce
- ½ teaspoon ground ginger
- ½ teaspoon garlic powder
- 2 cups cubed cooked chicken

1. Heat oil in wok or large skillet. Fry eggs until firm, breaking them into small pieces. Reserve 2 tablespoons onion for garnish. Add remaining onions and bamboo shoots to oil, stirring constantly.
2. Add cooked rice, stirring until rice is coated with oil and heated through.
3. Add soy sauce, ginger, garlic powder and chicken. Cook, stirring lightly, 5 minutes more or until chicken is heated through.

BEEF TERIYAKI

The sherry-soy marinade adds flavor as well as tenderizing to a less expensive cut of meat.

Makes about 36 appetizers.

- 1 top round steak (about 1½ pounds), cut 1-inch thick
- ½ cup dry sherry
- ¾ cup soy sauce
- 3 tablespoons bottled steak sauce
- 2 tablespoons sugar
- 2 cloves garlic, crushed
  8-inch bamboo skewers*

1. Pierce steak deeply all over with a fork; place in shallow non-metal dish.
2. Combine sherry, soy sauce, steak sauce, sugar and garlic in small bowl. Pour about ⅓ over steak; cover. (Reserve remaining marinade for dipping.) Refrigerate several hours or overnight, turning steak once or twice.
3. Cut meat into long, thin slices about ⅛-inch thick; thread accordion-style on bamboo skewers; brush with marinade. Place on rack over pan.
4. Broil, 2 to 3 inches from heat, 1 minute; turn; broil 1 minute longer. Serve with reserved marinade.
Soak in water before using to prevent excess charring.

HONG KONG CHICKEN

Bake at 350° for 1½ hours.
Makes 4 servings.

- 1 broiler-fryer (about 3 pounds)
- ¼ cup water
- ¼ cup dry sherry
- ¼ cup soy sauce
- ¼ cup honey
- 2 teaspoons seasoned salt

1. Cut chicken into quarters; arrange in a single layer in a 13×9×2-inch baking dish.
2. Mix water, sherry, soy sauce, honey and seasoned salt in a small bowl; pour over chicken, turning to coat on all sides; cover. Marinate chicken in refrigerator about 4 hours or overnight.
3. About 2 hours before serving time, remove chicken from refrigerator; let stand at room temperature 30 minutes, then drain; reserve marinade. Arrange chicken, skin-side up, on rack over broiler pan or in a shallow baking pan with a rack. Brush generously with part of the marinade.
4. Bake in a moderate oven (350°), basting with remaining marinade every 20 minutes, 1½ hours or until chicken is tender and deep golden brown.

●●●